AF271330

COMBAT ROLES
3
Anti-Armour Warfare

Previous page:
PT-76 light amphibious tank, mounting a 76mm gun. Although largely replaced by BMP in the Soviet Army, it is still found in other Warsaw Pact armies. *Novosti*

Below:
The British Abbot 105mm gun uses the same chassis as FV432. It and the M108 will eventually be replaced by the British/German/Italian SP70 155mm howitzer. *MOD*

COMBAT ROLES

3

Anti-Armour Warfare

CHARLES MESSENGER

03DA25

LONDON

IAN ALLAN LTD

The components of anti-armour warfare: from the air the 'tank busting' fixed and rotary wing aircraft, here the A-10 Thunderbolt II *(top)* and Hind-D *(centre)*; from the ground the tank, Challenger *(bottom)*, and *(back jacket)* artillery and infantry. *P. R. March; Tass; R. Adshead; Novosti; Bundesministerium der Verteidigung.*

US M60A1 main battle tank. Although this is now being replaced by M1 Abrams, several are still deployed in Germany in the A3 configuration with integrated fire control. *Author*

First published 1985

ISBN 0 7110 1396 9

All rights reserved. No part of this book may be reproduced or transmitted in any form or by any means, electronic or mechanical, including photo-copying, recording or by any information storage and retrieval system, without permission from the Publisher in writing.

© Charles Messenger 1985

Published by Ian Allan Ltd, Shepperton, Surrey; and printed by Ian Allan Printing Ltd at their works at Coombelands in Runnymede, England

Contents

Glossary and Abbreviations

ACV	Armoured command vehicle	IFF	Identification friend or foe
AFV	Armoured fighting vehicle	IFV	Infantry fighting vehicle
APC	Armoured personnel carrier	IGB	Inner German Border
APDS	Armour-piercing discarding sabot	II	Image intensification
APHE	Armour-piercing high explosive	IR	Infra-red
APSE	Armour-piercing special effects		
Arty	Artillery	KE	Kinetic energy
ATAF	Allied Tactical Air Force		
ATGW	Anti-tank guided weapon	MACLOS	Manual command to line of sight
ATk	Anti-tank	MBT	Main battle tank
AVLB	Armoured vehicle-launched bridge	Med	Medical
		MICV	Mechanised infantry combat vehicle
BAOR	British Army of the Rhine	MP	Military Police
BE	Belgian	MLRS	Multiple launch rocket system
Bn	Battalion		
Bty	Battery	NBC	Nuclear, biological, chemical
Bundeswehr	The army of the FRG	NL	Netherlands
		NORTHAG	Northern Army Group
CBU	Cluster bomb unit		
CE	Chemical energy	Offr	Officer
CENTAG	Central Army Group	OMG	Operational manoeuvre group
CEV	Combat engineer vehicle	ORATM	Off-route anti-tank mine
C³I	Command, control, communications, intelligence	PGM	Precision guided munition
CONUS	Continental US	Pl	Platoon
Coy	Company	PVO	Vojska Provivovozdusnoj Oborony (Soviet Air Defence troops)
DF	Defensive fires		
Div	Division	RCM	Radio countermeasures
		RDM	Remotely delivered mine
Engr	Engineer	Recce	Reconnaissance
		Regt	Regiment
FAC	Forward air controller		
FGA	Fighter ground attack	SACLOS	Semi-automatic command to line of sight
FOFA	Follow-on force attack		
FOO	Forward observation officer	SADARMS	Sense-and-destroy armor system (US)
FPF	Final preventitive fire	SAM	Surface-to-air missile
FRG	Federal Republic of Germany	Sect	Section
FS	Fin-stabilised	Sig	Signals
		SP	Self-propelled
GE	German		
GSFG	Group of Soviet Forces, Germany	Tk	Tank
		TVD	Theatre of Operations (Soviet)
HE	High explosive		
HEAT	HE anti-tank	UHF	Ultra high frequency
HEP	HE piercing		
HESH	HE squash head	VHF	Very high frequency
HF	High frequency		
HHC	Head and Headquarters Coy	2IC	Second in command

Fig 1   Salient details of a tank. (This represents no particular tank in service.)

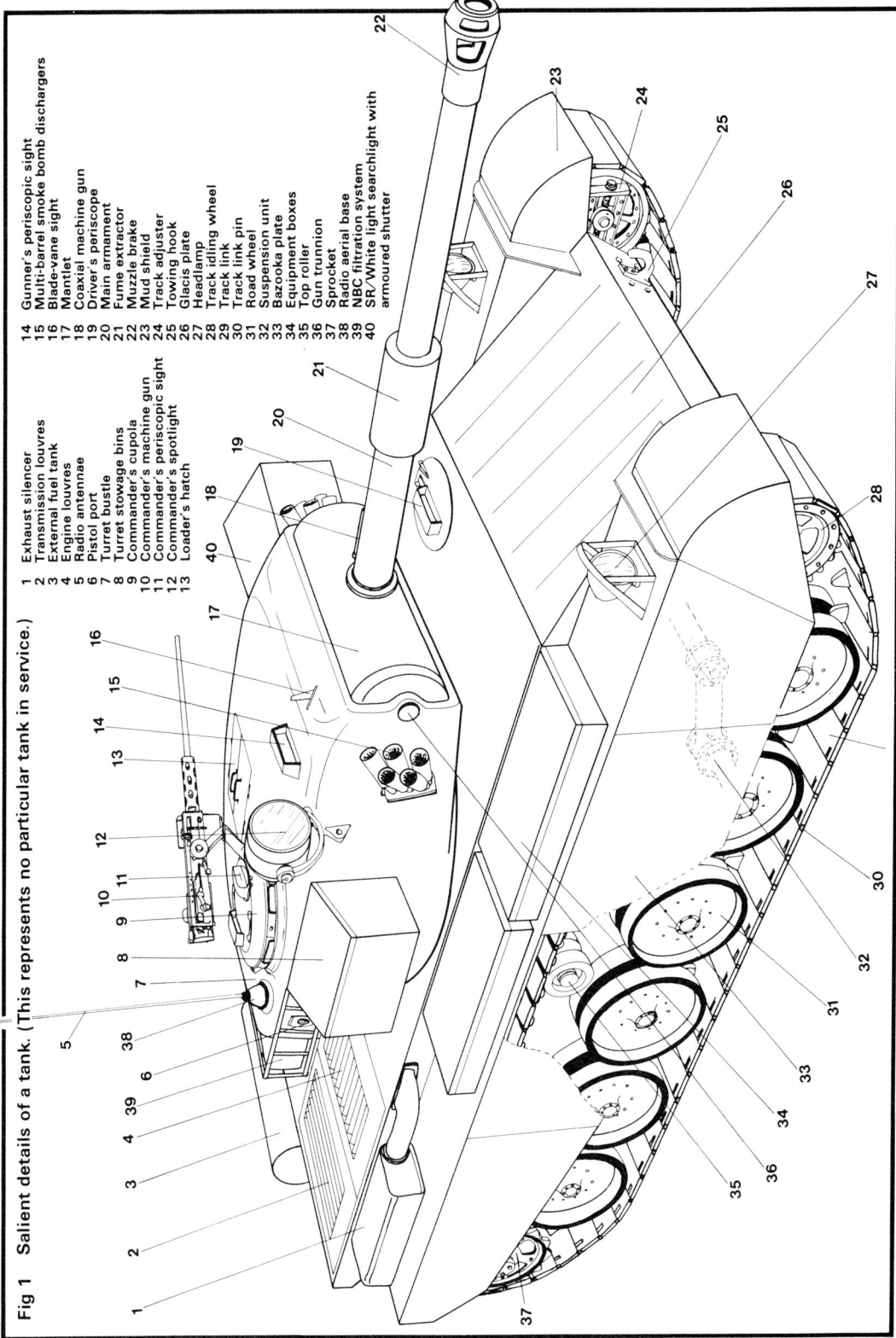

1	Exhaust silencer.
2	Transmission louvres
3	External fuel tank
4	Engine louvres
5	Radio antennae
6	Pistol port
7	Turret stowage bins
8	Turret bustle
9	Commander's cupola
10	Commander's machine gun
11	Commander's periscopic sight
12	Commander's spotlight
13	Loader's hatch
14	Gunner's periscopic sight
15	Multi-barrel smoke bomb dischargers
16	Blade-vane sight
17	Mantlet
18	Coaxial machine gun
19	Driver's periscope
20	Main armament
21	Fume extractor
22	Muzzle brake
23	Mud shield
24	Track adjuster
25	Towing hook
26	Glacis plate
27	Headlamp
28	Track idling wheel
29	Track link
30	Track link pin
31	Road wheel
32	Suspension unit
33	Bazooka plate
34	Equipment boxes
35	Top roller
36	Gun trunnion
37	Sprocket
38	Radio aerial base
39	NBC filtration system
40	SR/White light searchlight with armoured shutter

Introduction

The tank made its debut on the battlefield on 15 September 1916. That it did so was in an effort to break the deadlock of trench warfare, which had been brought about by the quick firing artillery piece, magazine rifle and the machine gun. By the end of World War 1 it was seen as a means of restoring mobility to the battlefield and became the cornerstone of the theories of mechanised warfare which were developed between the wars. The German Blitzkrieg campaigns of 1939–42 confirmed the theories; in almost every theatre of war the tank was dominant in the land battle. At the same time, in order that other arms could keep up with the tank on the battlefield, a family of armoured fighting vehicles (AFV) was spawned. Armoured personnel carriers (APC) for the infantry, self-propelled artillery and specialist engineer vehicles were all very much part of the order of battle by 1945.

In the 40 years that have followed the end of World War 2, the AFV has remained predominant in spite of competition from the helicopter and the anti-tank guided weapon (ATGW). The Arab-Israeli and Indo–Pakistan wars have helped to confirm this, but it is in Europe that the main focus of attention lies. It is here that the major battles will take place should a major global conflict ever break out again, and the two potential protagonists, the Warsaw Pact and the North Atlantic Treaty Organisation, regard the use of armour as vital to their plans. The major AFV producing countries of the world, with the exception of Israel, come from these two power blocs, and concepts and designs are set within the context of mechanised warfare in Europe, particularly the Federal Republic of Germany, which is known in NATO terms as the Central Region.

This book aims to show the methods and means by which the anti-armour battle might be fought in the Central Region should war break out tomorrow. It also takes note of current technological developments and leaves some thoughts as to how these might effect the anti-armour battle and, more especially, the future of the tank.

Charles Messenger

The Setting

Historically, the Low Countries were always considered to be Europe's battle ground. Since 1945, however, this has moved east and, should a future war break out, the major fighting will take place on the territory of the Federal Republic of Germany. On either side of the FRG's border with the German Democratic Republic are positioned two military alliances, the North Atlantic Treaty Organisation and the Warsaw Pact, and, in the event of hostilities between the two, the West sees the Warsaw Pact as the probable aggressor.

In NATO parlance the Federal Republic is known as the Central Region. It has a frontage of over 500 miles, running from the River Elbe in the north to the forests of Bohemia in the south. Its northern flank rests on the Elbe and the North Sea (Schleswig Holstein is considered part of the NATO command Allied Forces Northern Europe and is not included in the Central Region), while the southern flank is the border with neutral Austria and Switzerland. The northern part of the Region consists of the lowlands of Lower Saxony where the country is generally flat and in many places wet, although south of Hannover the landscape becomes more rolling. Two rivers run from north to south through the area, the Leine and, to its west,

the Weser. Then comes the Harz Mountains which jut into East Germany and are very wooded. The south of the region remains generally hilly and wooded. The state of Hesse, however, does not have a convenient north–south river line, but once in Bavaria, there is the River Danube.

The hilly nature of much of the Central Region obviously favours the defence, but this, combined with the forests, can be a two-edged weapon, since it makes the prospect of infiltration by an attacker that much more likely. The Soviets, however, used as they are to the flat open steppes which make up so much of Soviet Russia, regard the Central Region as being semi-mountainous requiring more refined tactical skills. They are also faced by another problem – the growing urbanisation of West Germany. A 1981 Bundeswehr study noted that there was a township of less than 3,000 inhabitants found in every 12sq km, and if natural

Below:
The wide open 'steppe' terrain in which these BMP-1s are operating, is very different to the typical North German countryside seen overleaf, with Chieftains and a Ferret moving forward on it. *Novosti; Author*

obstacles such as woods and waterways, as well as larger towns, are excluded, this is reduced to 7sq km. Towns and villages can be a very real brake on mobile operations, as many examples from World War 2 demonstrate, and again favour the defender. Nevertheless, there are areas where the country is generally open. In particular the North German Plain, the Fulda Gap northeast of Frankfurt-am-Main, the area around Würzburg and north of Munich are seen by NATO planners as likely avenues for Soviet main thrusts.

There is, however, another aspect with regard to the terrain which needs to be borne in mind. Another Bundeswehr study concluded that it was not possible to see out to ranges of more than 2,000m in more than 16% of the terrain of the

Central Region, and that 55% gave sighting ranges of less than 500m. This is particularly significant when considering the anti-armour battle, especially in terms of maximum effective ranges of weapon systems. To compound the problem, there is also the question of the weather. In winter, fog, snow and rain can restrict visibility to less than 1,000m at a height of 600m or more for up to 20 days in the month, and in summer there are certain to be some days when the same restriction applies, even at sea level.

Having looked at the ground on which the anti-armour battle will be fought, the weapon systems must now be examined.

Below:

NATO's Central Region showing the dispositions of Allied Forces Central Europe (AFCENT) and Soviet forces in East Germany and Czechoslovakia.

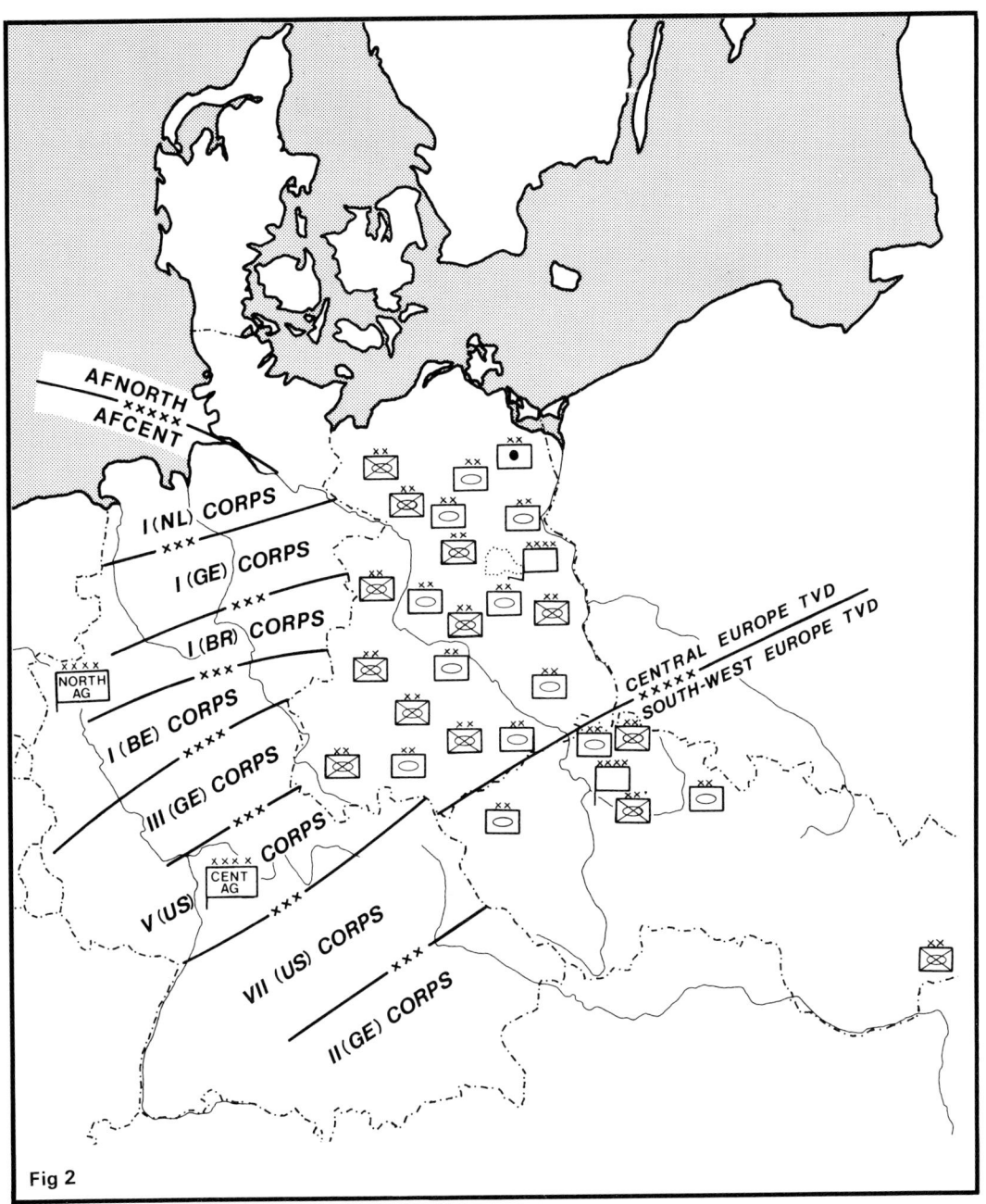

Fig 2

11

The Weapons

Anti-Armour Ammunition

Armour defeating ammunition comes in two basic types, kinetic energy (KE) and chemical energy (CE). KE rounds rely on mass and velocity to penetrate armour. Nowadays, the armour-piercing discarding sabot (APDS) round is the most widely used. This consists, as shown in Fig 3a, of a slug made of very dense material, which is enclosed in a pot or sabot. This is in three parts, but is held together by driving bands. Once the propellant is ignited, the projectile is driven up the barrel and, as soon as it leaves, the segments of sabot, with the driving bands worn away, break off, leaving the slug to fly on towards the target. Its high velocity is maintained because the force imparted by the propellant is now concentrated on a much smaller area.

Chemical energy rounds are of two natures – HESH and HEAT. HESH (high explosive squash head) has a relatively soft casing containing plastic explosive and a base fuse – Fig 3b. When it hits armour it forms a 'cowpat', which is detonated by the base fuse. This sends shock waves through the armour, which cause a scab and splinters of metal to break off from the inside face and these will fly round at high velocity around the interior of the armoured vehicle. HESH can also be used in the conventional high explosive role, which makes it a useful round to have. High explosive anti-tank (HEAT), on the other hand, is solely an anti-armour round, and works on an entirely different principle – Fig 3c. This is the hollow charge effect, first discovered by an American engineer in the 1820s. As shown in the diagram, the round consists of a hollow cone, with a metal liner covering the explosive charge. The probe in front of the round enables it to be detonated at the right 'stand off' distance. As the tip of the probe strikes the target, the actuator inside it trips the fuse, detonating the charge. This results in a stream of hot gas and molten metal from the liner, which penetrates the armour.

Up until recent years, all tank guns have been rifled in order to impart accuracy to the round through spin stabilisation. Rifled guns do, however, have a disadvantage in that the rifling wears comparatively quickly, thus causing inaccuracies, and this limits the force of the propellant charge. If it is too hot, greater wear will be inflicted on the rifling. In order to overcome this problem more and more tanks are now mounting smoothbore guns. The hotter charges that can be used mean that muzzle velocities can be increased, but stabilisation has to be achieved in another way, using fins – Fig 3d. Both APDS and HEAT rounds use fin-stabilisation, but with HESH it is difficult to achieve, and for this reason the British, unlike the other major tank producing nations, prefer to retain the rifled barrel, albeit firing fin-stabilised ammunition from it.

There is another category of anti-armour round, which combines both KE and CE. Known as high explosive piercing (HEP) or armour piercing high explosive or special effects (APHE, APSE), it relies on kinetic energy to penetrate the armour and then, once inside, explodes. Since it inevitably represents a compromise in design, it is not effective against MBTs, but is very useful against lighter armoured vehicles, especially APCs.

Anti-Armour Weapon Systems

Both the Warsaw Pact and NATO appreciate that there is no one dominant anti-armour weapons system, but rather that there are several different types of weapon, each with advantages in particular circumstances, and that they combine together in a family.

The Main Battle Tank

The characteristics of the tank are its powerful gun – nowadays linked to sophisticated fire control systems, capable of engaging enemy armour out to ranges of 3,000m – its armoured protection and mobility, as well as the flexibility provided by its radio communications. While all nations generally agree that firepower is the most important characteristic, there is much debate over protection and mobility, and which should be given the

Fig 3

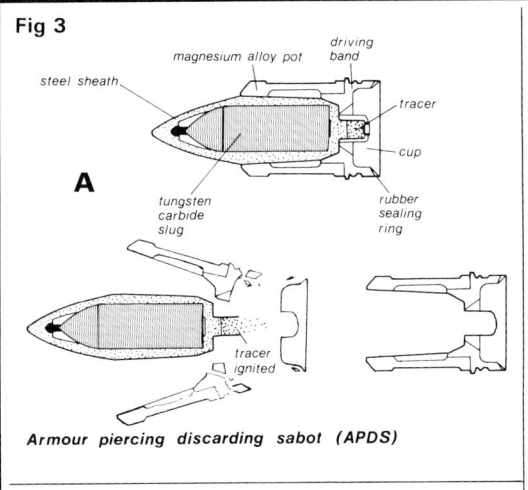

A

steel sheath
magnesium alloy pot
driving band
tracer
cup
tungsten carbide slug
rubber sealing ring
tracer ignited

Armour piercing discarding sabot (APDS)

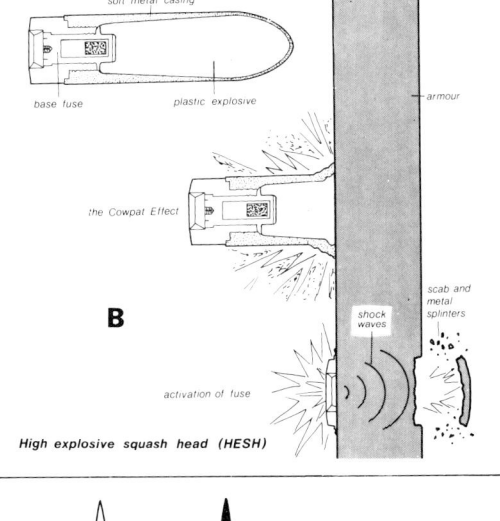

B

soft metal casing
armour
base fuse
plastic explosive
the Cowpat Effect
scab and metal splinters
shock waves
activation of fuse

High explosive squash head (HESH)

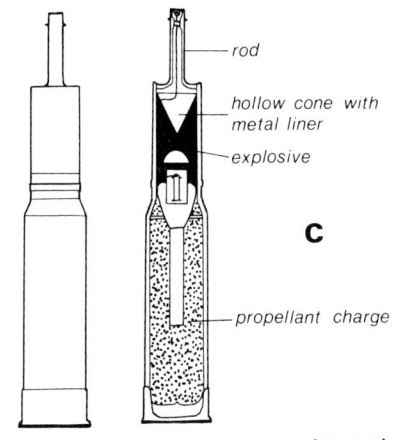

C

rod
hollow cone with metal liner
explosive
propellant charge

High explosive anti-tank (HEAT)

D

sabot
rod penetrator
fins
propellant charge
detonator

Armour piercing discarding sabot fin stabilised (APDSFS)

Anti-Armour Weapon Ranges		
M72, LAW 80, RPG-16	300m	MBT side attack only
Carl Gustav	500m	MBT side attack only
T-12 Anti-tank gun	1,000m	MBT side attack only
20–30m cannon	1,500m	light armoured vehicles only
76mm, 73mm AFV guns	1,500m	MBT side attack only
MILAN, 'Spandrell' ATGW	2,000m	
105mm, 115mm tank guns	2,000m	
HOT, 'Sagger-B' ATGW	3,000m	
120mm, 125mm tank guns	3,000m	
57mm, 2.75in air-to-surface rockets	3,500m	
TOW, Swingfire ATGW Hellfire	4,000m	
120mm mortar with PGM	7,000m	
AS-7 'Kerry' ASM	10,000m	
Maverick ASM	22,500m	
155mm howitzer with PGM	30,000m	

Above:
(a) APDS – the pot or sabot breaks off as the projectile leaves the muzzle of the gun. The steel sheath covering the slug shatters on impact with the target.
(b) HESH
(c) HEAT
(d) APDSFS.

greater emphasis. The British and Israelis believe that protection is the more important, whereas the Americans, Germans and French have put the emphasis on mobility. The Russians, on the other hand, believe that low silhouette makes an important contribution to protection, as well as saving weight, thus enhancing mobility. There are penalties to be paid for this. For a start, this makes the crew compartment very cramped and, indeed, the Soviets have had for many years to lay down a maximum height for tank crewmen. The other problem is over gun depression. Whereas Leopard

Main Battle Tank Armour Thicknesses

For obvious reasons, details on armour thicknesses on the most modern generation of MBTs are highly classified. Nevertheless, the thicknesses on the Soviet T-62 given below give a good indication as to where tank designers place the emphasis.

Plate	Thickness (mm)	Degree of slope to vertical
Glacis Plate	102	60
Front lower plate	102	54
Side Upper	79	0
Side Lower	15	0
Rear	46	0
Engine Deck	31	90
Belly	20	90
Turret front	242	0
Turret sides	153	5
Turret rear	97	0
Turret top	40–60	90

Points to Note

1 The lower side armour is much thinner than the upper side because of the protection provided by the road wheels. Side protection is further enhanced by the use of bazooka plates.
2 The belly armour is too thin to withstand the latest generation of belly attack mines.
3 The greater the slope to the vertical the more protection against KE projectiles is enhanced.
4 Protection is further increased by the addition of external bins, spare track links (normally mounted on the glacis plate) and reactive armour, such as the Israeli Blazer concept.

2, Challenger and M1 Abrams have a maximum depression of 10°, T-64 and T-72 can only achieve 5°. The implication of this is that NATO tanks, when in a firing position behind a crest can cover much more of the ground in front of them, as Fig 5 shows. A further drawback is that ammunition stowage is restricted, and Soviet tanks' ammunition stowage capacity is on average some 20% less than that of their NATO counterparts.

Priority of armoured protection is always given to the front of the tank – the glacis plate in front of the driver and the turret. Next come the sides and belly (to guard against mine attack) and finally the top and the rear, which in all MBTs apart from the Merkava houses the engine. In the past, designers have been able to make significant savings in weight by making the top of the tank comparatively thin in terms of armour. This, however, is now likely to change with the advent of precision guided munitions (PGM) such as the US Copperhead laser-directed 155mm artillery round and the Thomson-Brandt 120mm precision-guided mortar bomb. The potential capability of these high trajectory weapons to attack the tank from above will be a significant design factor in the next tank generation.

There are a number of different types of armoured protection which are used.

Right:
Anti-armour engagements – 1 tank v tank.

Below:
Gun depression – both tanks are in hull down positions and maximum gun depression below the horizontal is shown. M1 Abrams is able to engage targets at a much shorter range than T-64 because of its greater depression.

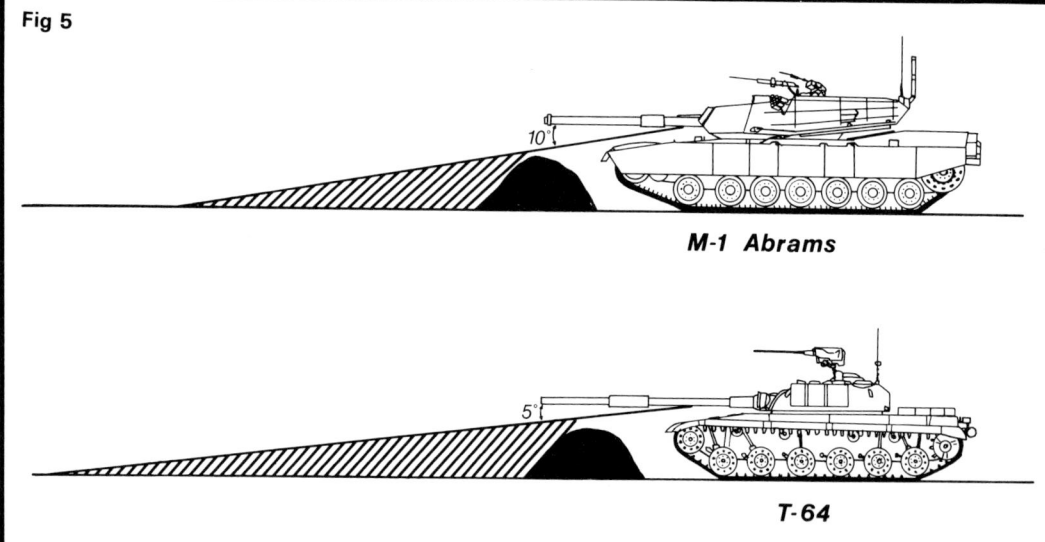

Fig 5

10°

M-1 Abrams

5°

T-64

Fig 4

ANTI-ARMOUR ENGAGEMENTS

TANK V TANK

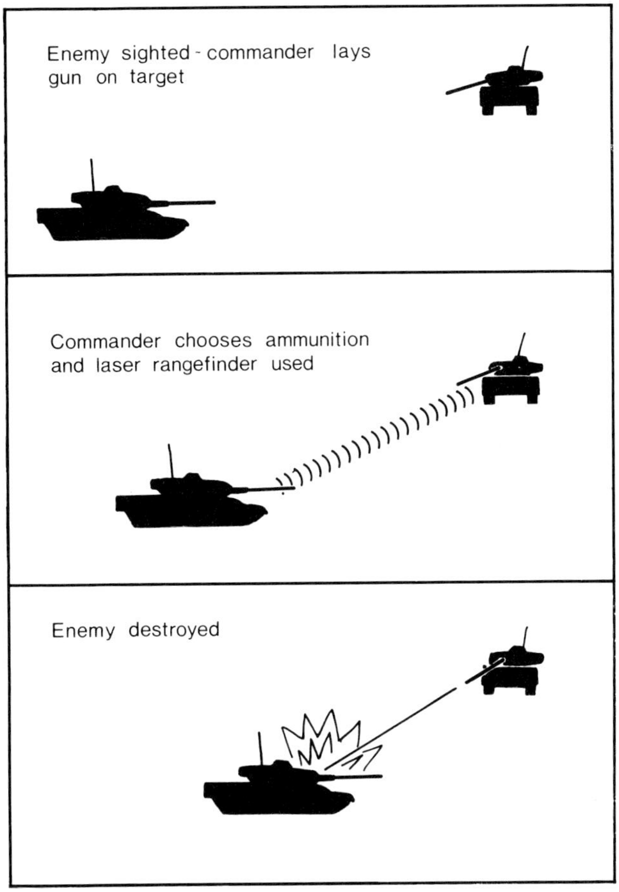

Commander
Spots tank through
his sight, identifies
as enemy.
Uses turret traverse
and gun elevation
controls to bring
target into gunner's
sight picture.
Gives out fire order,
detailing ammunition
type and description
of target.

Gives order to fire

If target hit, orders
cease fire and reports
details of engagement
on radio.

Gunner
Lays aiming mark onto
target, activates
laser rangefinder and
reads off range.

Feeds range and ammunition
type into ballistic computer.
Makes fine lay onto target.

Fires gun and watches for
strike on target (indicated
by a bright flash)

If target is missed, gunner
will shout out intended
correction, and commander will
amend if he disagrees.

Gunner fires.

Loader

Selects ammunition type from
ready round bin and loads.

Selects another round
and reports gun loaded.

Loads round and reports loaded.

Enemy sighted - commander lays
gun on target

Commander chooses ammunition
and laser rangefinder used

Enemy destroyed

1. Tanks will always travel with the main
armament loaded if combat is likely. If the
commander considers that the type of round
in the breech is unsuitable for the target, he
will fire it off first before loading with the
correct type.

2. Chieftain and Challenger are different from
other tanks in that their 120mm rounds come
in two parts – projectile and bag charge. The
charges are stowed in special fireproof
containers, which reduces the danger of a fire
in the tank if it is hit, and prevents the turret
floor from becoming cluttered with brass
cases. This can become an especial problem
when the tank is closed down and sealed
against an NBC threat. Nevertheless, loading
times are only fractional slower than with the
more traditional 'all in one' round.

Above:
T-80, the latest version of T-72, which is distinguishable by the smoke grenade dischargers mounted on the front of the turret. This has ceramic armour and an integrated fire control system, including laser rangefinder, incorporated. *Author*

Solid armour The traditional armour, usually made of a steel alloy. Obviously the thicker the armour the more effective it is, but there is the penalty of weight to be paid. Also, while effective against KE attack it is more easily defeated by CE rounds.

Spaced armour Better protection against CE rounds is provided by spaced armour, which, as the name implies, is two thicknesses of armour with a space between them. The most common example of this is the bazooka or skirting plates which are fitted to the sides of most Western tanks.

Laminated armour This bonds together thicknesses of armour made of different materials. Chobham armour, which is now being used in both Warsaw Pact and NATO tanks, is based on this principle, although the materials used are classified information.

Appliqué armour Apart from incorporating protection within the body of the hull and turret, another means is 'bolt on' or appliqué armour. This is literally bolting armour onto the hull and turret in order to increase protection. This can be in the form of additional armour plates, track links or even tool bins. The Israelis have used the latter

to develop a new form of 'bolt on' armour which they call 'Blazer'. This is 'reactive armour' consisting of a number of metal boxes which contain explosive. When a projectile strikes the box it sets off the explosive which blows outwards, thus reducing the effect of the projectile. Blazer seems to have proved itself during the Israeli invasion of Lebanon in 1982.

The combination of mobility and protection gives the tank what the Israelis call 'battlefield mobility' or the ability to move about the battlefield under fire. This, however, pertains more to the weapons platform than the weapon itself. It is the gun, together with its fire control system and ammunition, which makes the tank a formidable weapon in the anti-armour role. The gun itself and the types of anti-armour ammunition used have already been discussed, but much of their effectiveness depends on the ability of the crews to acquire, engage and destroy targets quickly. This is the role of the fire control system.

The normal tank turret crew is made up of the commander, gunner and sometimes a loader/radio operator as well, although certainly the Soviets now use an auto-loader instead. Both commander and gunner have a number of optical systems. In the case of the commander, there is a periscope sight set into the roof of the turret. This is made up of a unity window, which gives him a wide field of view, and a magnified sight with a graticule pattern superimposed on it. Also, he has a number of episcopes set around his turret, which give him 360° vision when he is closed down. Most tanks now have a system whereby they commander can rotate his own turrent independently of the main turrent. Then, having identified a target and lined his sight up with it, he can automatically bring the main turrent round so that the gunner also has the target in his sight picture. The commander then lays down the type of ammunition to be used and hands over to the gunner. In the past, there were a number of reasons why the first round fired would not hit the target. To begin with, commanders had to estimate the range to the target, no easy task to do accurately at ranges out to 2,000m. To overcome this, and provide a precise range, the latest generation of MBTs use laser rangefinders. A number of other factors, including the round's behaviour in flight and the angle of tilt of the trunnions, will also affect accuracy. In order to allow for these, fire control computers are now widely used. These are programmed using ballistic range table figures and, combined with sensors to measure trunnion tilt, enable the gunner to lay his gun very much more accurately than in the past. The net result of this is that the main battle tank of today is capable of a 90% probability of acquiring and destroying a target with one round within 10 seconds.

Above:
Challenger in desert garb. Although some 7,000kg heavier than Chieftain, its 1,200bhp engine gives it a top speed of 60kph as opposed to Chieftain's 48kph. This view shows to good effect the slab-like Chobham armour. *MoD*

Left:
Like TOW, the Euromissile HOT has also been modified with a wider warhead diameter as HOT 2 in order to combat recent improvements in armour. *Author*

Anti-Tank Guided Missiles

The guided missile used in the anti-armour role began to come into service in the late 1950s. Because of its higher accuracy and longer effective range compared with those of the tank guns of the time, there was a strong body of opinion in the early 1970s asserting that the missile had sounded the death knell of the tank. The evidence for this was the initial Egyptian successes with the Soviet 'Sagger' missile in the 1973 Yom Kippur War and the impressive results obtained by US helicopter-mounted ATGW against North Vietnamese tanks in early 1972. In the event, more sober minds prevailed and ATGW was recognised as an important member of the anti-armour family, but not decisive in its own right.

Because of their relatively slow velocities ATGWs have HEAT warheads. The enhanced effectiveness of Chobham-style armour has, however, made the current size of warhead too small to guarantee destruction of a tank, especially if it is struck head on. Therefore, the diameter size is being increased, especially on the US TOW missile and German Milan.

ATGW relies on command guidance for the missile to strike its target. This means that the operator has to give the missile commands. For first generation missiles this was done through manual command to line of sight, which meant that the controller had first to gather the missile, and then manoeuvre it by means of a 'joystick', which sent signals down a wire attached to the missile, onto the line of sight between his eye and the target and maintain it on this line. The problem was that, as the French found in Algeria, under the stress of battle operator performance quickly declined. The current generation therefore has a semi-automatic system known as SACLOS – semi-automatic command to line of sight. The controller merely has to keep his sight on the target and the missile will automatically fly along this line. The incorporation of thermal

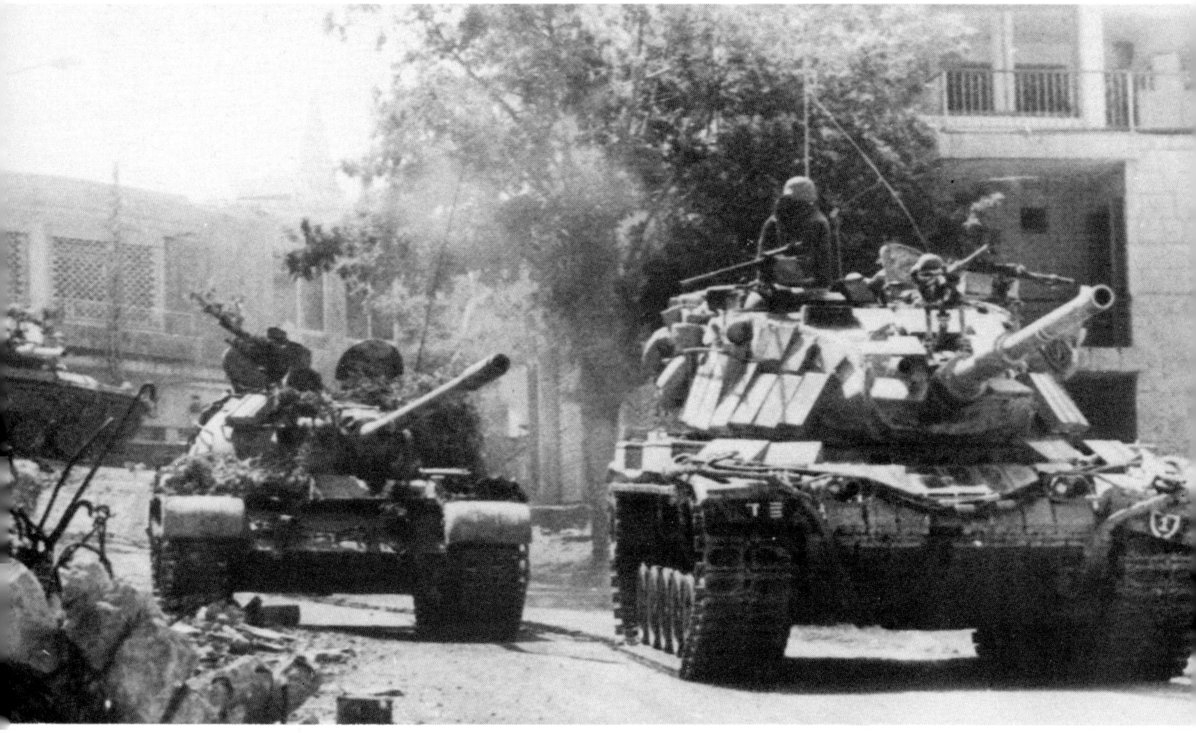

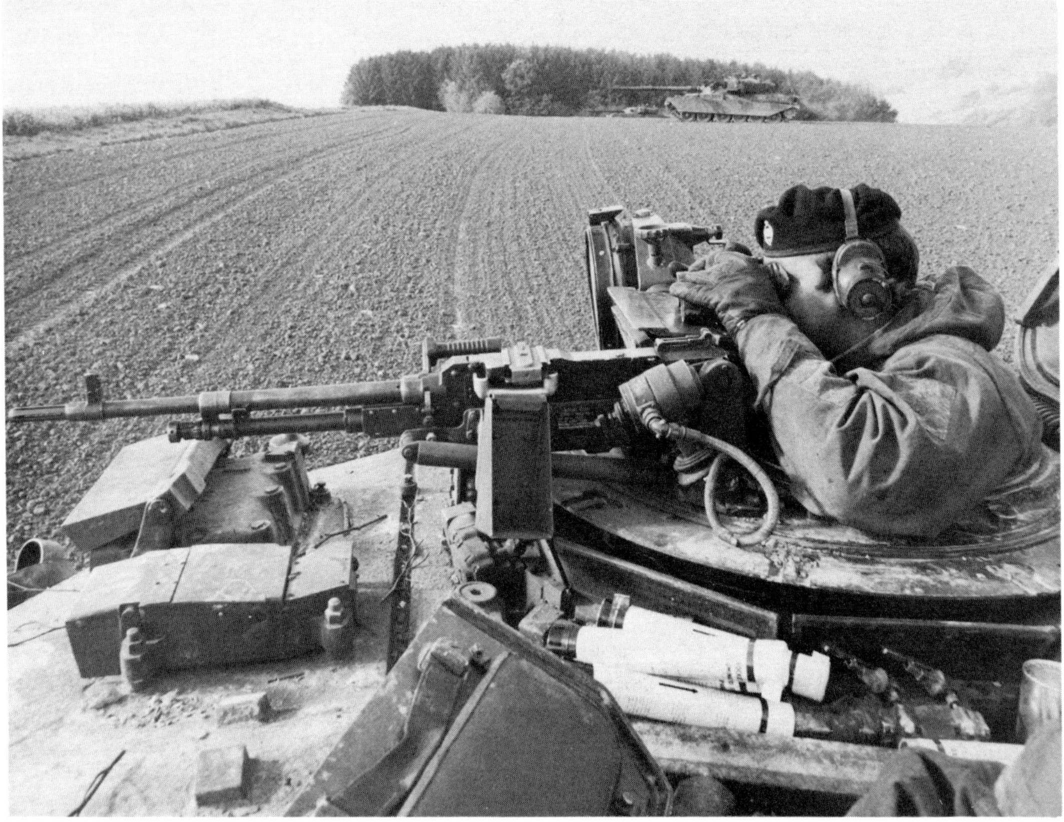

Above left:
In order to enhance armour protection, the Israelis have developed 'Blazer' armour, which consists of metal boxes bolted onto the turret, as shown by this Israeli M60 passing an abandoned Syrian T-54/55 in the Lebanon in June 1982
Associated Press

Left:
Chieftain commander's turret showing episcopes, 7.62mm MG and spotlight. These vehicles are turret down behind a ridge. They will move forward to hull down positions to engage enemy armour and then reverse back and 'jockey' into a fresh fire position. See Fig 18. *Author*

Above:
Chieftain. Although it entered British Army service in 1966, continual modifications have ensured that it remains a match for the latest Soviet tanks. *Soldier*

imaging also enables ATGW systems to be used during the hours or darkness or in conditions of poor visibility.

ATGW exists in two categories, long and medium range. The former, of which the British Swingfire and US TOW – whose range has been increased from 2,000 to 3,750m – are examples, cover systems which can reach out to 4,000m. The medium range ATGW usually has a range of 2,000m and is the infantry's main form of anti-armour defence.

ATGW is employed in three ways. It can be ground or vehicle-mounted or used in helicopters.

Anti-Tank Guns
Towed and self-propelled anti-tank guns have given way to ATGW within NATO armies. The same is true to an increasing extent in Warsaw Pact armies, although Soviet airborne divisions still rely on guns in the shape of their 100mm and ASU-85 self-propelled gun. The main problem with towed guns is crew vulnerability on the modern battlefield, while self-propelled anti-tank guns suffer from limited gun traverse, with major adjustments having to be made by turning the vehicle on its tracks.

Hand-Held Rocket Launchers
Both NATO and the Warsaw Pact deploy a large number of these with their infantry. These have ranges of up to 600m and are ideal against armour in closer country. They have HEAT warheads, but these are not large enough to attack successfully the frontal armour of the modern MBT, and hence the infantryman will normally try to aim for the side or rear.

Artillery
Most artillery guns have an anti-armour round, albeit not in much quantity since field artillery would only engage armour directly in an emergency. NATO countries normally use HEP or HESH,

Above:
Milan being operated by an Italian soldier. He merely has to keep the aiming mark in his periscopic sight on the target for the missile to hit. *SHAPE P.R.*

Left and below left:
Striker ready to fire and with the missile controller using the separated mode. *Author*

Below:
The result of an ATGW strike. *Oerlikon-Bührle Ltd*

Above right:
Anti-armour engagements – 2 ATGW helicopter v tank.

Fig 6

ATGW HELICOPTER V TANK

Observation Helicopter
Observing above cover

Spots tank, identifies it as
enemy, and radios details on
tank type and location to
attack helicopter.

Drops back behind cover

Resumes observation

Attack Helicopter
Hovering behind cover

Rises above cover, observer/GW controller
activates firing circuits, locates target
and lays aiming mark in his sight on it.
Fires missile and maintains aim on target
until missile strikes.
Drops back behind cover

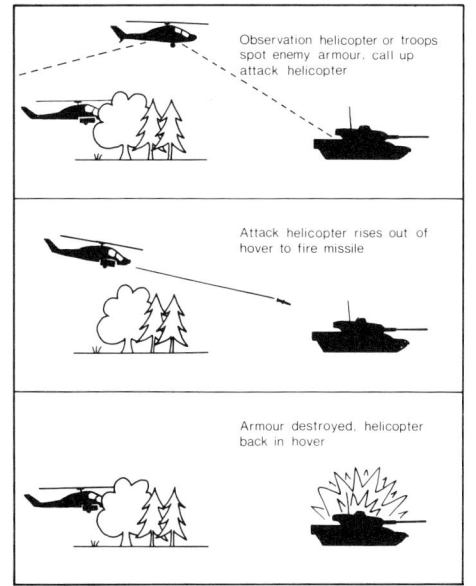

Observation helicopter or troops
spot enemy armour, call up
attack helicopter

Attack helicopter rises out of
hover to fire missile

Armour destroyed, helicopter
back in hover

A HOT or TOW missile spends the first 700m
of its flight adjusting onto the line of sight
between the controller and target. The missile
takes some 16 seconds to fly to its maximum
range of 4000m, and during this time the
helicopter is very vulnerable because it is at
the static hover and an easy target for any low
level air defence weapon. The introduction of
the mast mounted sight will radically reduce
this danger in that the helicopter can remain
covered from observation while firing a
missile.

Below:
Westland Lynx firing HOT. *Westland*

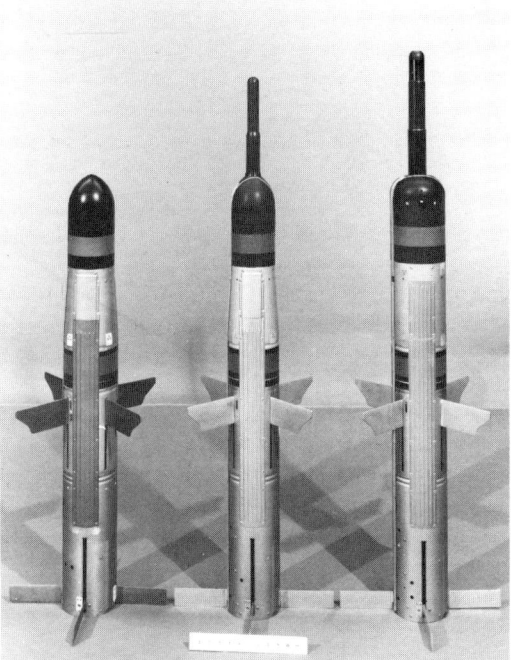

Above:
Another means of delivering ATGW. Here TOW missile launchers as fitted to the Lynx helicopter. *Soldier*

Left:
TOW ATGW missiles. Left is the ordinary missile, centre is improved TOW with a 5in diameter warhead and right TOW 2 with 6in warhead. Increased warhead size is to combat recent improvements in tank armour. *Hughes Aircraft Co*

Below:
The British Army's latest hand-held anti-armour weapon, LAW 80. It has an effective range of up to 500m, and incorporates a spotting rifle, with magazine of six rounds. It can be telescoped for ease of carrying and the launcher tube is discarded after firing. *HQ BAOR PR*

while the Warsaw Pact relies on HEAT. In the future, with the advent of the PGM, artillery is likely to play a much greater part in the anti-armour battle. The first PGM, the US 155mm Copperhead round, has been under development for some years. An observer well forward uses a laser target designator to indicate the target and merely gives the guns a map square in which to

Above:
Exercise 'Lionheart' 1984 – a British Carl Gustav team engaging an M1 Abrams. The man in the centre is carrying his NBC overboots on his back. *Author*

Below:
Soviet T-12 100mm anti-tank gun, being towed by the MTLB tractor. There is a battalion of these guns in each Motor Rifle Division. *Author*

23

Fig 7

PRECISION GUIDED ARTILLERY/MORTAR ROUNDS V TANKS

Forward Observer

Spots target, identifies as enemy and radios back its rough location in terms of a map grid square.

Switches on his laser designator and aims it at the target. The laser beam is reflected off the target and picked up by the sensor in the nose of the round/bomb, guiding it towards the target.

Gun/Mortar Position

Grid square is fed into a computer, which provides elevation and bearing settings for gun/mortar. These are passed to the crew. Once gun/mortar is loaded and laid, order to fire is given. Radio message passed to Forward Observer informing him that the round/bomb is on its way.

In a conventional artillery/mortar shoot, the Forward Observer uses a laser range designator to obtain the range to the target and also takes a bearing on it (the latest generation of designators also give a read out of this as well). He passes this back, together with the location of the target. Normally one gun/mortar will fire and the observer will then pass back corrections on the fall of shot in order to get the rounds on target relative to his own position. The fire control computer, knowing the bearing and range of the target from the observer, can automatically calculate how these corrections should be converted in order to bring the guns, which are thousands of metres away from the observer, onto target.

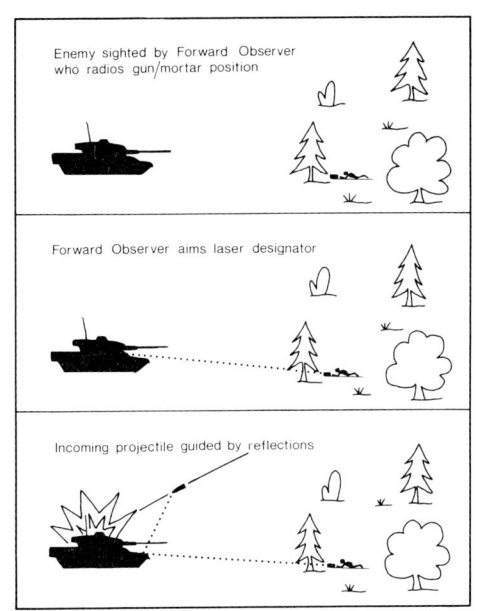

Enemy sighted by Forward Observer who radios gun/mortar position

Forward Observer aims laser designator

Incoming projectile guided by reflections

fire. Once the round gets close to the target, a laser sensor in it will pick up the reflection of the laser off the target and guide the round on to it. A similar system is being developed by the French firm of Thomson-Brandt for its 120mm mortar. Recently, the US has been working on a new type of anti-armour PGM which is called the 'sense-and-destroy armour system' (SADARMS). This does not require a forward observer and relies on radar to detect targets. The round contains three anti-armour sub-munitions, each with a radar sensor in it. They are ejected from the carrier shell by a time fuse and are supported by a parachute. The sensor, once it detects a target, locks on to it and guides the sub-munition down on to the top of it. Similar

Left:
Anti-armour engagements – 3 Precision-guided artillery/mortar v tank

Far left:
In order to combat minefields, some tanks are fitted with mine ploughs. Here is a Royal Engineers Centurion fitted with the Pearson mine plough. *HQ BAOR PR*

Below left:
The Multiple Launch Rocket System, being developed jointly by the USA, France, West Germany and UK, will not only enhance conventional field artillery, but can be used to lay scatterable minefields and fire anti-armour precision guided sub-munitions. *LTV Corporation*

Below:
FV432 with Ranger and Barmine laying systems. While the towed Barmine layer lays the anti-tank mines, anti-personnel mines are fired from the Ranger launcher. *Soldier*

systems are also being developed for the Multiple Launch Rocket System (MLRS) and for the US Air Force.

Above:
Harrier, seen here in a typical tactical operating site is very versatile in the anti-armour close support role. *Soldier*

Mines

The anti-tank mine remains a major threat to the tank, whether it achieves what is called a 'K-Kill', where the tank is knocked out completely, or an 'M-Kill', which disables the tank so that it cannot move, but can still use its gun. The traditional type of mine, which is represented by the US M15, the Soviet TM-46 and the British Mk 7, relies on blast, which will destroy the tracks and suspension, thus achieving an M-Kill. A heavier type is the US M21 which has a shaped charge effect, producing a self-forging fragment. The problem with these mines is that they are magnetic and hence easily detected, even though they have anti-handling devices which complicate clearance. Hence plastic mines, like the US M19, are now becoming widespread. A further development is the off-route anti-tank mine (ORATM). This relies on a pressure tape placed across the likely route of the tank. Once this is crossed it triggers a hollow charge projectile, which is fired from the side, attacking the tank in the flank. In order to make detection more difficult, the Americans are now developing a refinement, replacing the tape with an acoustic sensor and infra-red fuse.

In the past, the major drawbacks of minefields have been the time taken to lay them and the danger that they will restrict the mobility of friendly forces. One solution to the latter is the incorporation of devices designed to deactivate the mine after a certain period of time. In terms of laying, a revolutionary development is the remotely delivered mine (RDM). This can be emplaced by artillery, MLRS or helicopter, and gives significant flexibility in that the mines can be laid only when the enemy is actually threatening a particular sector.

Air Delivered Anti-Armour Munitions

Apart from the attack helicopter armed with ATGW, the AFV is also under threat from aircraft in the close support and interdiction roles. The two main anti-armour weapons employed by aircraft are the cluster bomb unit (CBU) and unguided rockets. The former usually contain a mix of anti-armour and anti-personnel sub-munitions, while the latter are mounted in pods. These are ideal against concentrations of AFVs. 20mm and 30mm cannon are also very effective against lightly armoured AFVs. The concept of the tank busting aircraft – so successful in World War 2 – has been revivified in NATO terms by the introduction of the A-10 Thunderbolt II. Whether this slow moving fixed wing aircraft will be able to survive on today's battlefield remains a question that will only be answered by experience, but the proliferation of hand-held, throwaway SAM launchers does breed certain doubts.

The Threat

Ever since the formation of the North Atlantic Treaty Organisation in 1949 and that of its Eastern Bloc counterpart, the Warsaw Pact, in 1955, the threat of war between the two has existed. NATO has always considered the most likely scenario to be a Warsaw Pact invasion of the Federal Republic of Germany, and hence the NATO Central Region has concerned planners more than any other area. However, in order to formulate workable plans to counter this threat, it has and always will be necessary to define exactly what that threat is.

The Great Patriotic War of 1941–5 left an indelible scar on the Soviet Union in terms of ravages to the country and losses in manpower. It is understandable, therefore, that the USSR should be so worried about 'invasion'. At the same time, Marxist–Leninism has always regarded war as a legitimate revolutionary tool, especially if it is a 'justified war', which is defined as being either one of liberation of peoples from the bonds of capitalism, or as defence against attack, which can be interpreted – if need be – as launching a pre-emptive strike in much the same way as the Israelis did in 1956 and more especially in 1967. Indeed, it is this aspect which NATO views as the most likely reason for the Soviet Union deciding to invade the West, and it is noteworthy that Warsaw Pact manoeuvres place greatest emphasis on the counter-offensive, with defence *per se* having low priority in training. Consequently, taking these two factors together, the Soviet Union has long concluded that an invasion of Western Europe must be carried out in such a way as to achieve victory in the shortest possible time: although, obviously, whether the Soviets are likely to go to war is a matter of debate.

As a counter to the NATO doctrine of flexible response, the Soviets believe in having a demonstrable ability to win a war at any level – conventional, tactical nuclear or strategic nuclear. However, they are fully conscious of the NATO nuclear armoury, and indeed it has been the potential of this to inflict unacceptable damage on the Soviet Union and her satellites which has, more than any other factor, helped to maintain peace in Europe over the past 35 years. Therefore, should the Soviet Union feel compelled to go to war against the West, she wants to do so at the minimum cost to herself, which means achieving victory by conventional means alone. For this, surprise and speed are the essence.

Russia is well aware that it will take NATO forces in the Central Region time to deploy and set up their positions and that also NATO plans rely on having time enough to reinforce troops already stationed in the Federal Republic from outside. Hence, the Soviets would dearly like to gain initial strategic surprise and engage NATO troops in a classic encounter battle while they are still deploying from barracks. If this happened, NATO planners consider that they would have no more than 48 hours warning. On the other hand, the growing sophistication of surveillance and information processing systems make this difficult to achieve, even if the Warsaw Pact was to attempt to disguise its intentions through large-scale manoeuvres, which, in any event, in line with the 1972 Helsinki Agreement, have to be notified well in advance to NATO if above a certain size. Also, it would allow the Pact no time to organise its follow-up forces. Indeed, up until recently, NATO planners have worked on the premise that seven days' warning is a more likely scenario, with a further eight days required to deploy those forces based back in Russia itself. However, of late a third option has been receiving growing acceptance, that of a period of tension during which the Warsaw Pact would carry out its strategic build up, followed by a long delay, during which time NATO would begin to stand down its previously deployed forces, and finally the gaining of tactical surprise when it is believed that the NATO guard has been lowered.

If maximum advantage is to be gained from this initial surprise it is essential that the speed and momentum of the attack should be maintained. NATO forces must be given no chance to recover from the early shock of assault and, in order to keep the fighting conventional, the military objec-

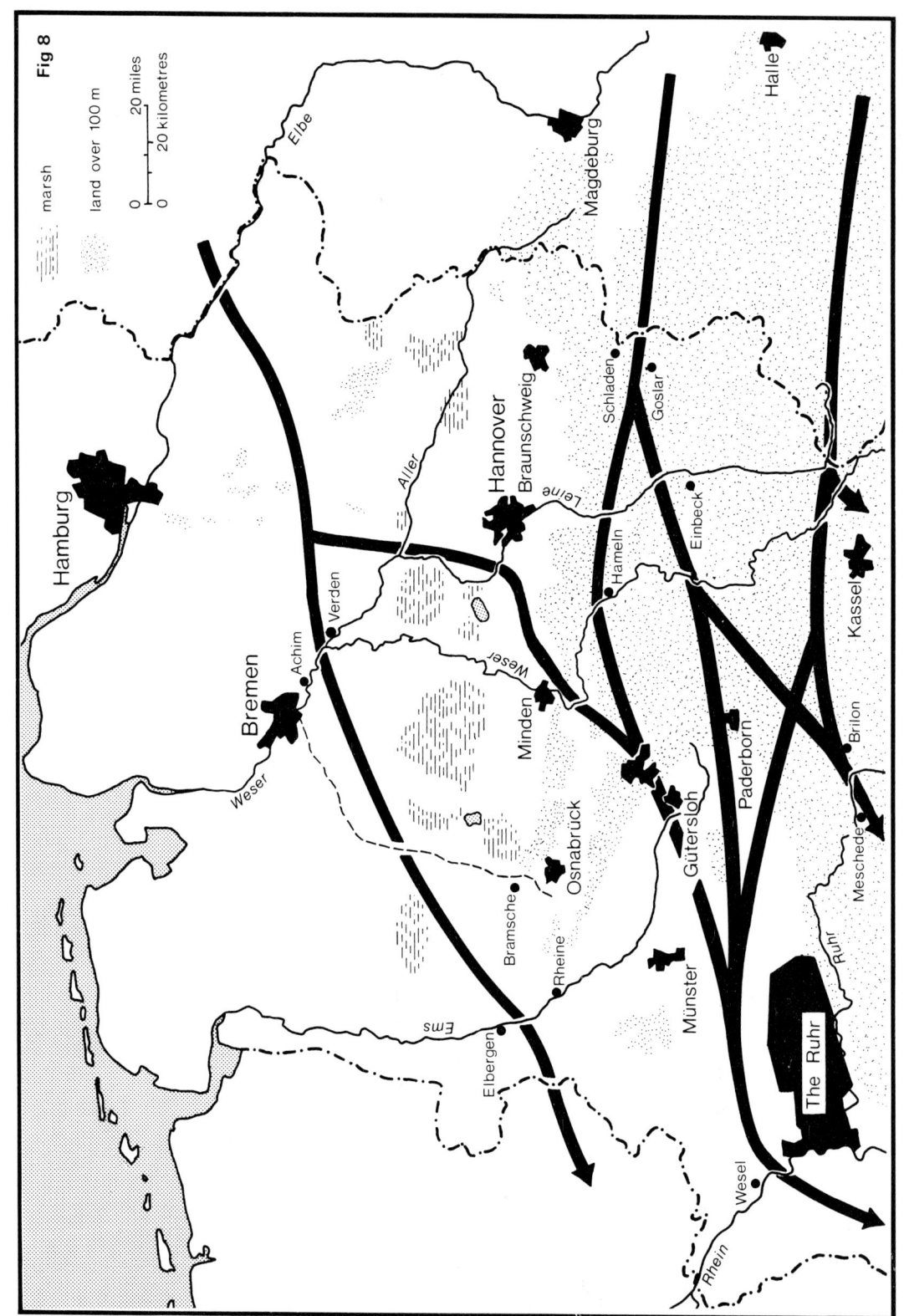

Fig 8

marsh

land over 100 m

20 miles

20 kilometres

0

0

Hamburg

Bremen

Weser

Achim

Verden

Aller

Elbe

Hannover

Braunschweig

Leine

Magdeburg

Halle

Schladen

Goslar

Einbeck

Hameln

Kassel

Weser

Minden

Osnabrück

Bramsche

Rheine

Ems

Elbergen

Münster

Gütersloh

Paderborn

Brilon

Meschede

Ruhr

The Ruhr

Wesel

Rhein

Fig 9

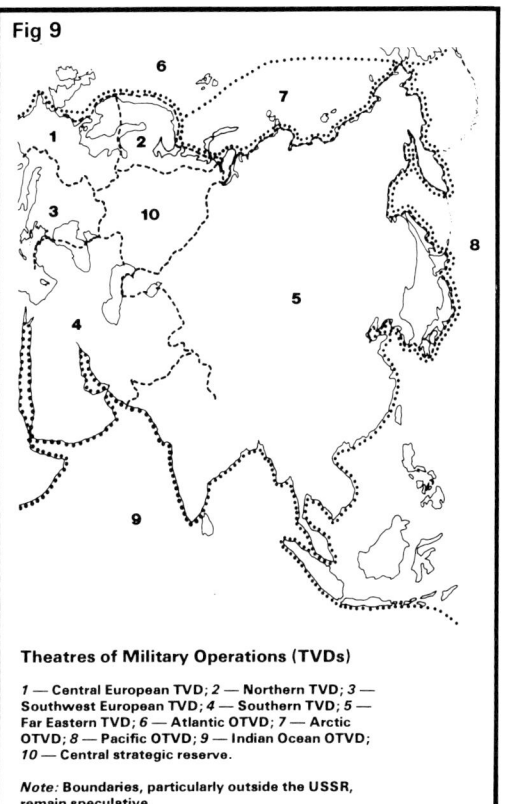

Theatres of Military Operations (TVDs)

1 — Central European TVD; *2* — Northern TVD; *3* —
Southwest European TVD; *4* — Southern TVD; *5* —
Far Eastern TVD; *6* — Atlantic OTVD; *7* — Arctic
OTVD; *8* — Pacific OTVD; *9* — Indian Ocean OTVD;
10 — Central strategic reserve.

Note: Boundaries, particularly outside the USSR,
remain speculative.

Group of Soviet Forces, Germany (GSFG)

The five armies of GSFG are organised as follows:

1st Guards Tank Army	Dresden
6th Guards Tank Division	Lutherstadt-Wittenberg
7th Guards Tank Division	Dessau-Rosslau
9th Tank Division	Riesa
11th Guards Tank Division	Dresden-Klotzsche
27th Guards Motor Rifle Division	Halle
2nd Guards Army	Furstenberg
16th Guards Tank Division	Neustrelitz
21st Motor Rifle Division	Perleberg
25th Tank Division	Vogelsang/Berlin
94th Guards Motor Rifle Division	Schwerin
3rd Shock Army	Magdeburg
10th Guards Tank Division	Krampnitz
12th Guards Tank Division	Neuruppin
47th Guards Tank Division	Hillersleben
207th Guards Motor Rifle Division	Stendal
8th Guards Army	Weimar-Nohra
79th Guards Tank Division	Jena
20th Guards Motor Rifle Division	Grimma
39th Guards Motor Rifle Division	Ohrduf/Thur
57th Guards Motor Rifle Division	Naumburg/Saale
20th Guards Army	Eberswalde
6th Guards Motor Rifle Division	Bernau
14th Guards Motor Rifle Division	Juterborg
35th Motor Rifle Division	Dobertiz

The headquarters of GSFG is at Zossen-Wunsdorf outside
Berlin and 30th Artillery Division is based at Potsdam.

Left:
**Possible Warsaw Pact axes of advance against
NATO's NORTHAG.**

Above:
The Soviet Theatres of Operations (TVDs).

tives must be achieved before the collective NATO
decision to 'go nuclear', which is likely to take time
in view of the democratic nature of the Alliance
and the awesome possible consequences inherent
in this step, can be made. As for the tools to carry
this out, the Soviet Union has since 1945 relied on
the traditional blitzkrieg recipe of mechanised
ground forces operating in conjunction with air
power to produce victory through dislocation
rather than wholesale destruction of the enemy
forces. Thus, as far as the ground forces are
concerned, the main element in their equipment is
the AFV, especially the tank.

Overall command of Warsaw Pact forces in the
Central Region in time of war is likely to be
exercised by the Supreme Command of the Warsaw
Pact at Lvov in Poland. The most important
element of the land forces is the Group of Soviet
Forces Germany (GSFG), which is made up of five
armies with a total of 20 divisions, 10 tank and 10
motor rifle, as well as an artillery division. This,

supported by its own integral strike aviation and
air defence assets (PVO), is permanently based in
the German Democratic Republic and would
provide the first strategic echelon in the Central
Europe Military Theatre of Operations (TVD) see
Fig 9. The East Germans could augment GSFG
with up to two tank and four motor rifle divisions.
In the southern part of the Central Region, there
are further Warsaw Pact forces stationed in
Czechoslovakia. These come under the Southwest
Europe TVD and are made up of four armies, two
Soviet and two Czech, with a total of six tank and
eight motor rifle divisions. Both TVDs also have
strategic strike aviation support – 24th Air Army in
the case of Central Europe and 4th Air Army for
Southwest Europe.

While it is likely that the majority of satellite
forces will be committed to the lines of communi-
cation and, more especially, in maintaining
internal security within their own national
territories, the Soviet Union herself has some 67
divisions positioned in her western military
districts and, although these are not at full strength,
unlike those described in the previous paragraph,
they can be brought up to wartime establishment
within a few days and would provide the second
strategic echelon.

For the purposes of this book it is proposed, however, to concentrate solely on GSFG as a means of illustrating the problems which face NATO with regard to the anti-armour battle.

The two basic elements of the Soviet ground forces are the tank and motor rifle divisions. While the former tends to be used to spearhead and support breakthrough along the main axis of advance, the Motor Rifle Division is used in closer country or against the stronger defensive positions, although recent organisational changes in both have made them more flexible than hitherto. In comparison to their Western counterparts both are very much more firepower intensive and lighter on manpower.

The Tank Division

In the past this was an inflexible organisation. Today there is no one standard order of battle for the Soviet tank division and often additional tank battalions or companies or motor rifle companies are added to the basic organisation given in Fig 10.

The Tank Regiment
See Fig 11.

Tank Division Motor Rifle Regiment
This is BMP equipped, as is all of the Motor Rifle Regiments in the Motor Rifle Division and has a different organisation to the normal Motor Rifle Regiment. See Fig 12.

Motor Rifle Division
See Fig 13.

BTR-60 Motor Rifle Regiment
See Fig 14.

Below:
The Tank Division.
Total personnel: 10,000 men (inc 1,000 offr)
Total vehicles: 328 MBTs, 57 BRDMs, 130 BMPs

Below right:
The Tank Regiment.
Total personnel: c1,000 men (inc 120 offr)
Total vehicles: 94 MBTs, 13 BRDMs, 14 BMPs

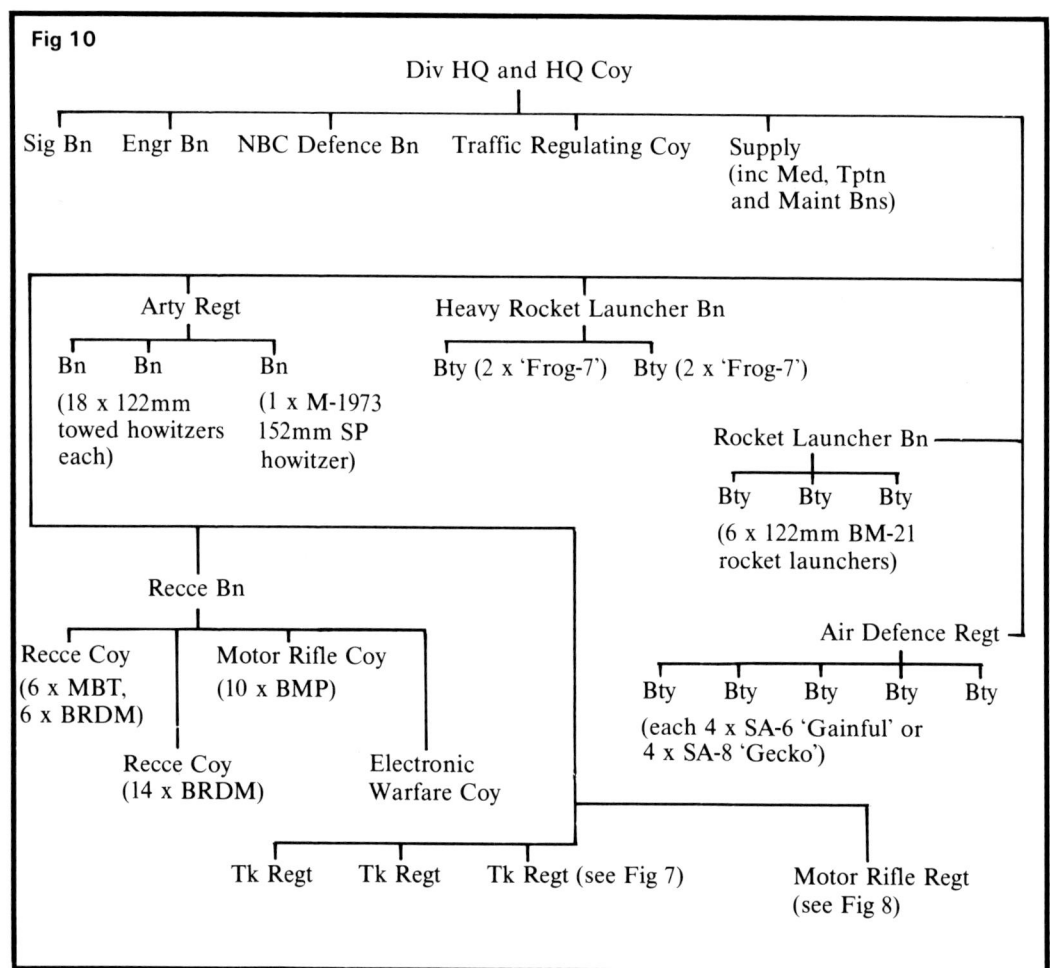

Fig 10

Equipment – AFVs

Main Battle Tanks

Soviet tank design came into its own during World War 2 with the appearance of the T-34, generally judged to be one of the outstanding tanks of the war, and its heavier counterpart the JS-III. Since then, with the T-54/55, T-62, T-64 and T-72, the Soviets have developed a series of MBTs, which is noted for the comparatively low silhouette, which makes them less of a target than their Western rivals, cramped crew conditions, but overall robustness.

Within GSFG the most common MBT found is the T-64. This was developed in the 1960s as a replacement for the T-54/55, and was first spotted by the West in 1970 when it was undergoing user trials, and was provisionally named M1970. It started to re-equip GSFG from 1975. Although its firepower is impressive, it suffers from automotive problems, being underpowered and having obsolescent running gear, and in some cases it is

likely to be replaced by the T-72. This was developed as a parallel project and, although very similar in many respects, it has a more powerful engine and simplified running gear. Apart from equipping Warsaw Pact countries, it has also been exported to the Middle East, and Syrian T-72s were in action against Israeli tanks during the 1982 Lebanese War. It is likely that more recent production models will have composite armour, similar to Chobham armour, on the hull front and sides, which gives them greater protection against chemical energy attack. T-72 has recently undergone an improvement programme, including the installation of a laser rangefinder. This new version is designated T-80.

The T-62, the most common tank in the Soviet armoury during the 1960s and 1970s, is still to be found in large numbers, and in the past 15 years has undergone improvements in firepower. The T-54/55, although somewhat obsolete, equips the independent tank battalion in the motor rifle division. Indeed, the point is worth making that

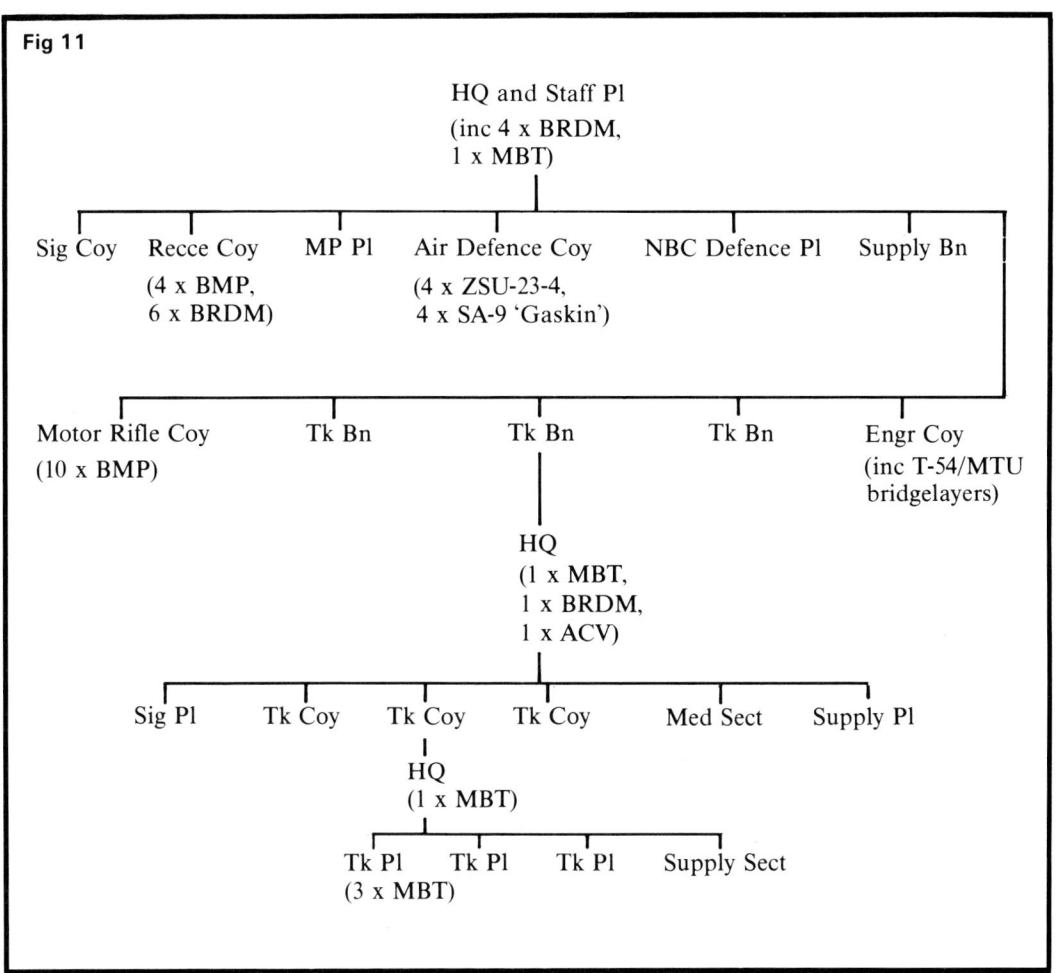

Fig 11

HQ and Staff Pl
(inc 4 x BRDM,
1 x MBT)

Sig Coy   Recce Coy   MP Pl   Air Defence Coy   NBC Defence Pl   Supply Bn
           (4 x BMP,   (4 x ZSU-23-4,
           6 x BRDM)   4 x SA-9 'Gaskin')

Motor Rifle Coy   Tk Bn   Tk Bn   Tk Bn   Engr Coy
(10 x BMP)   (inc T-54/MTU
                                             bridgelayers)

HQ
(1 x MBT,
1 x BRDM,
1 x ACV)

Sig Pl   Tk Coy   Tk Coy   Tk Coy   Med Sect   Supply Pl

HQ
(1 x MBT)

Tk Pl   Tk Pl   Tk Pl   Supply Sect
(3 x MBT)

Fig 12

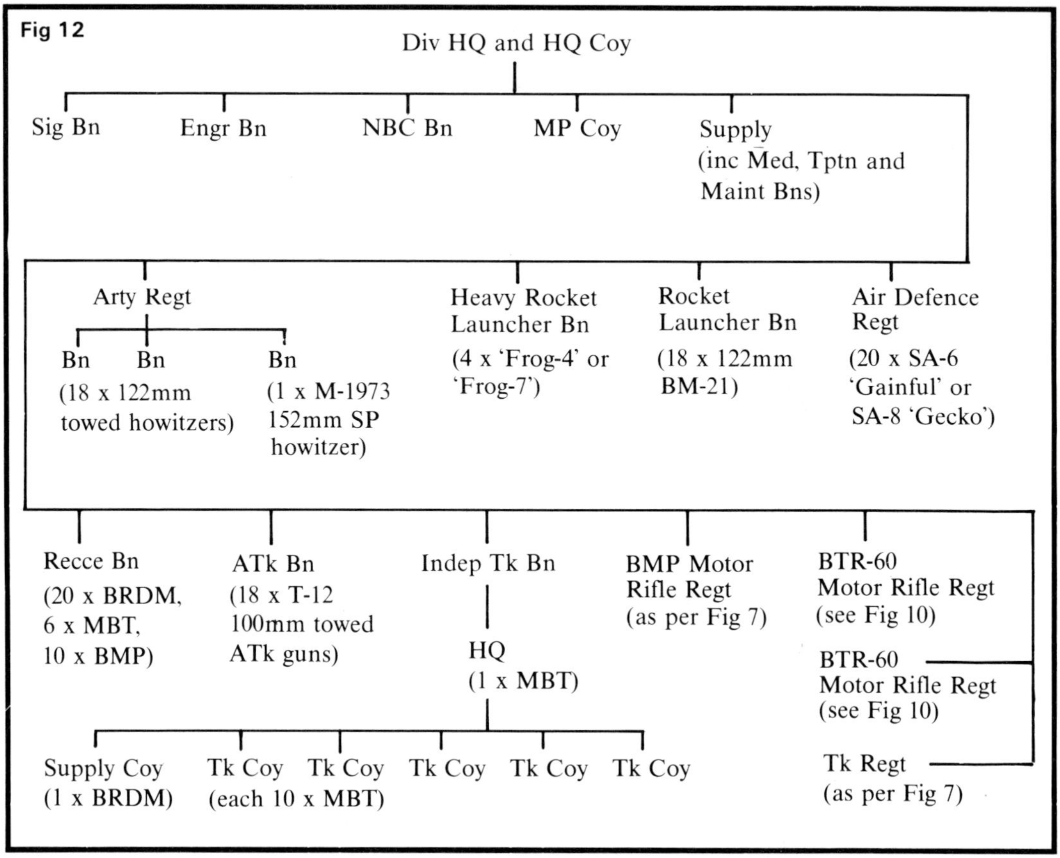

Div HQ and HQ Coy

Sig Bn	Engr Bn	NBC Bn	MP Coy	Supply (inc Med, Tptn and Maint Bns)

Arty Regt			Heavy Rocket Launcher Bn (4 x 'Frog-4' or 'Frog-7')	Rocket Launcher Bn (18 x 122mm BM-21)	Air Defence Regt (20 x SA-6 'Gainful' or SA-8 'Gecko')
Bn Bn (18 x 122mm towed howitzers)		Bn (1 x M-1973 152mm SP howitzer)			

Recce Bn (20 x BRDM, 6 x MBT, 10 x BMP)	ATk Bn (18 x T-12 100mm towed ATk guns)	Indep Tk Bn	BMP Motor Rifle Regt (as per Fig 7)	BTR-60 Motor Rifle Regt (see Fig 10)

HQ
(1 x MBT)

BTR-60
Motor Rifle Regt
(see Fig 10)

Supply Coy (1 x BRDM)	Tk Coy Tk Coy Tk Coy Tk Coy Tk Coy (each 10 x MBT)	Tk Regt (as per Fig 7)

Above:
The Motor Rifle Regiment.
Total personnel: c2,100 men (inc 200 offr)
Total vehicles: 40 MBTs, 24 BRDMs, 106 BMPs

Left:
**T-54/55, which first appeared in the late 1940s.
Nevertheless, it is still used in the Independent
Tank Battalion of the Motorised Rifle Division.
Armed with a 100mm rifled gun, it fires APHE
and HEAT ammunition.** *Author*

Below left:
**T-62 was the first Soviet tank to mount a
smoothbore gun, the 115mm. It is now used
mainly in second-line units.** *Author*

Top right:
**The Motor Rifle Division
Total personnel: 12,000 men (inc 1,100 offr)
Total vehicles: 265 MBTs, 117 BRDMs, 116
BMPs, 186 BTR-60PBs**

Above right:
**T-64, with its 125mm smoothbore gun is
currently the mainstay of the Group of Soviet
Forces Germany, although it is likely to be
replaced, at least in part, by the modified T-72, T-
80.** *Author*

Right:
**The original version of T-72, which has been
widely seen, not just in Warsaw Pact Countries,
but the Middle East as well.** *Author*

Fig 13

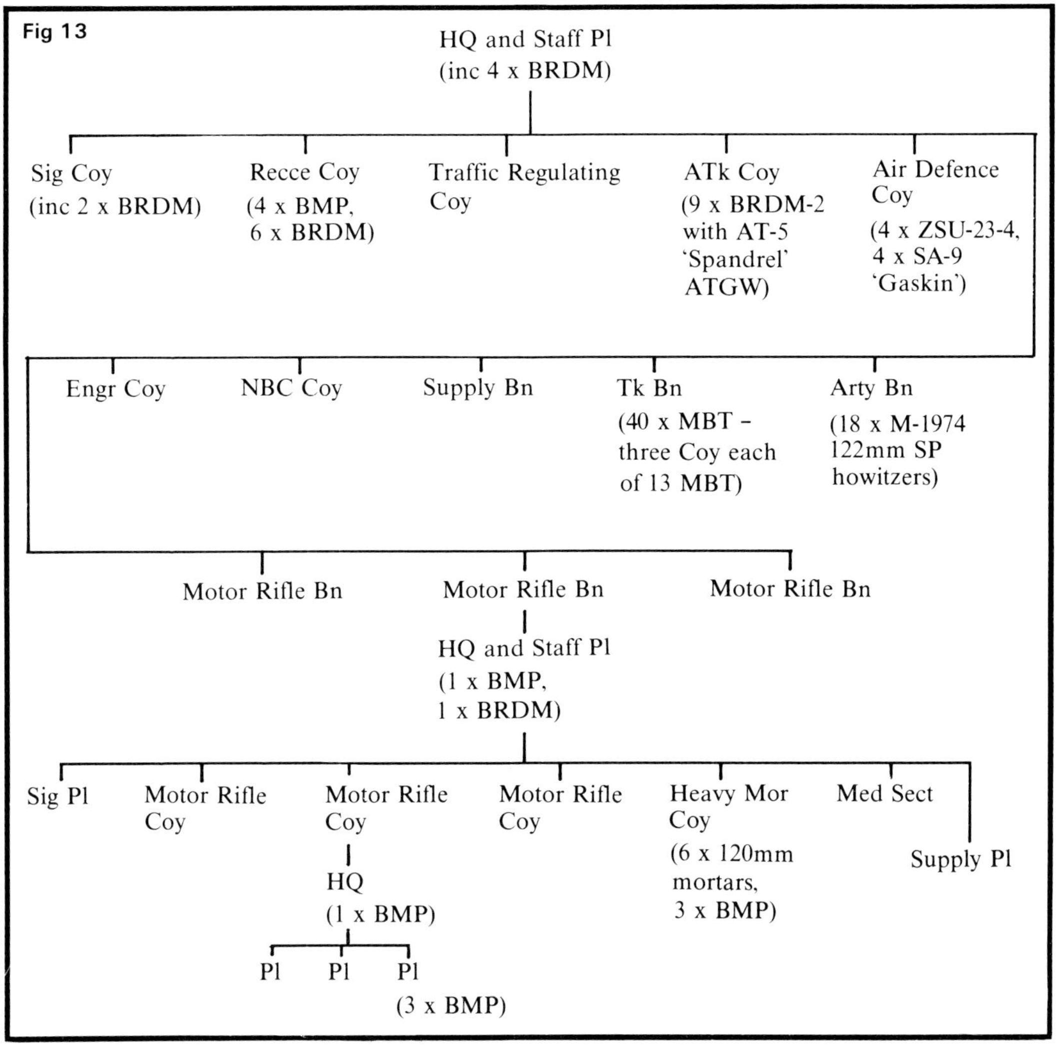

```
                                    HQ and Staff Pl
                                    (inc 4 x BRDM)
        ┌───────────────┬───────────────┼───────────────┬───────────────┐
   Sig Coy          Recce Coy      Traffic Regulating   ATk Coy         Air Defence
   (inc 2 x BRDM)   (4 x BMP,      Coy                  (9 x BRDM-2     Coy
                    6 x BRDM)                            with AT-5       (4 x ZSU-23-4,
                                                         'Spandrel'      4 x SA-9
                                                         ATGW)           'Gaskin')

      ┌───────────────┬───────────────┬───────────────┬───────────────┐
   Engr Coy        NBC Coy         Supply Bn        Tk Bn            Arty Bn
                                                     (40 x MBT –      (18 x M-1974
                                                     three Coy each   122mm SP
                                                     of 13 MBT)       howitzers)

      ┌───────────────────────┬───────────────────────┐
   Motor Rifle Bn         Motor Rifle Bn          Motor Rifle Bn
                               │
                          HQ and Staff Pl
                          (1 x BMP,
                          1 x BRDM)
   ┌──────┬──────────┬──────────┬──────────┬──────────┬──────────┐
 Sig Pl  Motor Rifle  Motor Rifle  Motor Rifle  Heavy Mor   Med Sect
         Coy          Coy          Coy          Coy
                         │                      (6 x 120mm            Supply Pl
                        HQ                      mortars,
                        (1 x BMP)               3 x BMP)
                    ┌────┼────┐
                   Pl   Pl   Pl
                   (3 x BMP)
```

the Soviets are loath to scrap obsolete equipment and when estimating relative tank strengths between East and West it is tempting to forget this fact.

Apart from the organisations already shown a tank regiment of 95 or 125 MBTs is also found at Army level.

Within the next two or three years, a new Soviet tank is likely to enter service. Like the T-64 and T-72, it has a three-man crew and is armed with a 125mm smoothbore gun and automatic loader. It is also certain to have composite armour, and is believed to have an engine of some 1,000hp and hydro-pneumatic suspension.

Armoured Reconnaissance Vehicles
The workhorse of Warsaw Pact ground reconnaissance is the BRDM scout car. BRDM-1 with an open turret entered service in 1959, and the

33

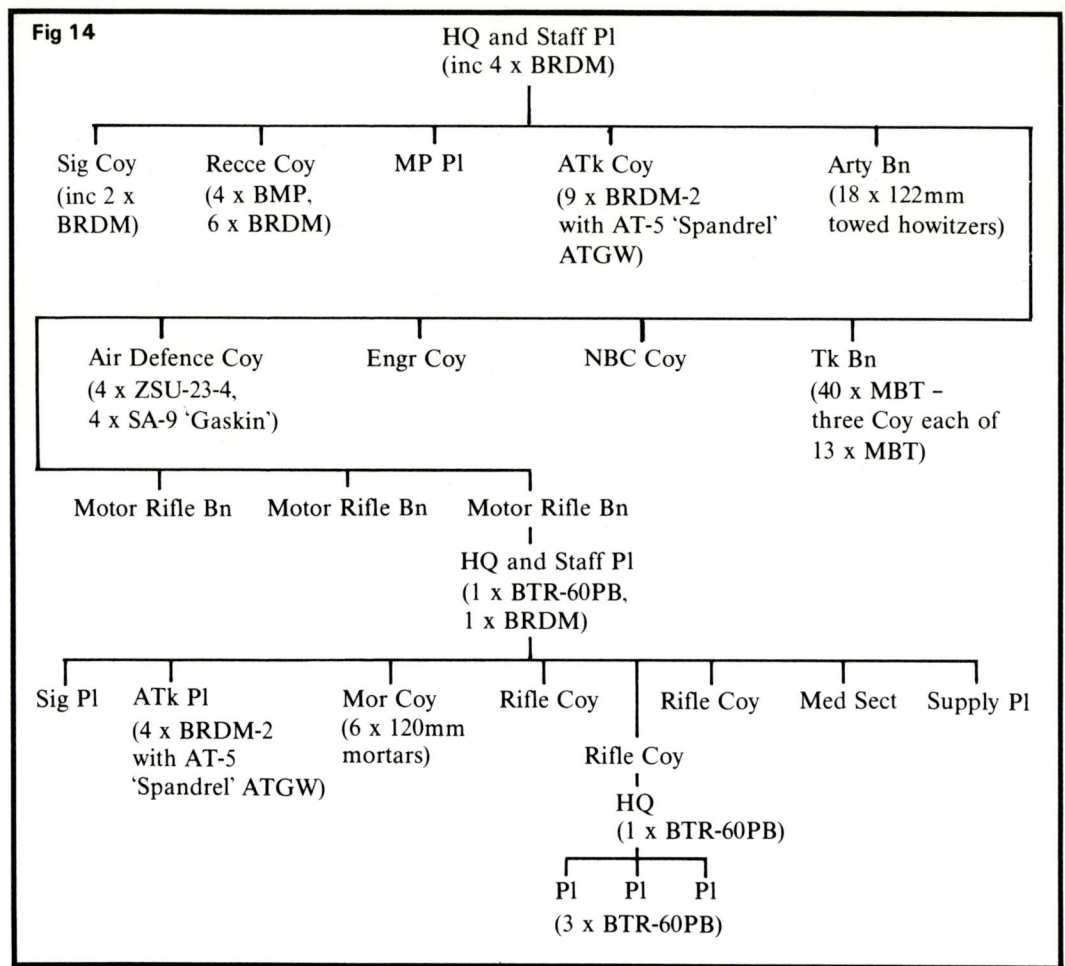

Fig 14

HQ and Staff Pl
(inc 4 x BRDM)

Sig Coy
(inc 2 x
BRDM)

Recce Coy
(4 x BMP,
6 x BRDM)

MP Pl

ATk Coy
(9 x BRDM-2
with AT-5 'Spandrel'
ATGW)

Arty Bn
(18 x 122mm
towed howitzers)

Air Defence Coy
(4 x ZSU-23-4,
4 x SA-9 'Gaskin')

Engr Coy

NBC Coy

Tk Bn
(40 x MBT –
three Coy each of
13 x MBT)

Motor Rifle Bn   Motor Rifle Bn   Motor Rifle Bn

HQ and Staff Pl
(1 x BTR-60PB,
1 x BRDM)

Sig Pl   ATk Pl
(4 x BRDM-2
with AT-5
'Spandrel' ATGW)

Mor Coy
(6 x 120mm
mortars)

Rifle Coy   Rifle Coy   Med Sect   Supply Pl

Rifle Coy

HQ
(1 x BTR-60PB)

Pl   Pl   Pl
(3 x BTR-60PB)

BRDM-2, with enclosed turret, a few years later. It is fully amphibious and has 2x2 retractable cross-country wheels. Although the basic vehicle in both cases is armed with only machine guns – 12.7mm or 7.62mm anti-aircraft and 14.5mm and 7.62mm hull/turret – an ATGW version exists in anti-tank units mounting 'Snapper', 'Swatter' or 'Spandrel' ATGW launchers. There is also an NBC reconnaissance version. The Hungarians, Bulgarians, Czechs and Poles also use the Hungarian FUG, which is very similar in configuration to the BRDM, with the FUG-63 being open-topped and the FUG-70 turreted.

Mechanised Infantry Combat Vehicle
The Russians were the first to introduce what is now an increasingly common form of infantry combat vehicle, when BMP-1 came into service in 1967. The previous APC concept envisaged mechanised infantry dismounting to fight and using their vehicles merely as battlefield taxis. With BMP, however, came a vehicle from which the infantry could actually fight and, armed with a 73mm smoothbore gun and 'Sagger' ATGW launcher, it is a formidable armoured fighting vehicle. It can also be seen as a means of increasing the momentum of the advance since the infantry will be forced to dismount less often. The more recent model, BMP-2, is recognisable by the more prominent sharp prow at the front and the longer deflector shroud at the rear, both modifications introduced to improve the amphibious capability. An airborne MICV, with the same armament as BMP, is BMD.

Armoured Personnel Carriers
The BTR-60PB eight-wheeled APC is still very much the basic AFV of the motor rifle division, and was introduced in its original straight BTR-60P configuration with open top and no turret in 1961 as the replacement for BTR-152, which is still to be seen with second-line units. The 'PB' version came into service in the mid-1960s and is totally enclosed with a turret mounting a 14.5mm machine

Left:
The BTR-60 Motor Rifle regiment.
Total personnel: c2,000 men (inc 200 offr)
Total vehicles: 40 MBTs, 36 BRDMs, 93 BTR-60PBs

Above:
The Soviet BMP-1 mechanised infantry combat vehicle. The base for the 'Sagger' ATGW can be seen on top of the barrel of the 73mm smoothbore gun. The crew is three (commander, gunner in the turret, driver) and eight infantrymen. BMP-2 has a much more pronounced prow. *TASS*

Below:
Backbone of Soviet reconnaissance, the BRDM. It will normally be supported by tanks. *Author*

gun. The equivalent in use in the Czech and Polish armies is the jointly developed OT-64 SKOT, which mounts two 'Sagger' ATGW launchers. Two other APCs, both tracked, which are now only occasionally seen, are the Soviet BTR-50 and its Czech counterpart the OT-62 TOPAS, which is also used by the Poles.

Equipment – Supporting Arms

While the main concern of the NATO ground forces will be to bring any Warsaw Pact attack to a halt by destroying a sufficient number of its AFVs, the range of supporting weapons which the Pact can bring to bear in order to impede and indeed

Top:
BTR-60PB, which is found only in Soviet motor rifle divisions. Fourteen infantrymen can be carried in the hull. *Author*

Above:
The Czech equivalent on BTR-60 is the OT-64 Skot. This is the 64C(2) with 14.5mm in an air defence turret. It can carry 18 infantrymen. *Author*

Top right:
The Czech OT-62B with 82mm recoilless gun mounted on the right hand turret. It is used in many of the satellite armies. *Author*

Above right:
The BTR-152 wheeled APC, although obsolescent, is still used in second line and training units in the Soviet Army. *Author*

assist in the destruction of NATO's defences cannot be ignored.

Artillery

The Soviet Union has long regarded artillery as the 'Queen of the Battlefield' and the weight of fire which Soviet artillery can bring down on enemy troops is impressive. In essence, there are four main types – towed field artillery, self-propelled field artillery, missiles and rockets.

Towed Artillery
Unlike NATO, the Soviets still place great reliance on towed artillery and this is evidenced by the two

122mm towed artillery battalions found within both the tank and motor rifle divisions. Within GSFG this the D-30 gun/howitzer, which has a high rate of fire of eight rounds per minute. Within satellite armies and in Soviet second-line formations, the M-38 122mm howitzer and M-43 152mm howitzer will also be found, along with the M-37 152mm howitzer. However, at Army level will be found an additional artillery brigade. This includes two battalions of 130mm M-54 guns and, in the combined army as opposed to tank army, one battalion of 152mm M-37 or the later M-55 D-20 gun/howitzer.

Self-Propelled Field Artillery
Whereas by 1945 the self-propelled artillery piece had become an important equipment in the majority of Western armies, the Russians did not introduce it until the early 1970s when the M-1973 152mm and M-1974 122mm came into service. The latter is employed with BMP motor rifle regiments, while the former is to be found within the divisional artillery of both tank and motor rifle divisions, as well as a further battalion being found in the tank army artillery brigade. Recently the Soviet Union has also deployed a 203mm self-propelled howitzer, which is capable of firing both nuclear and conventional rounds, and is probably retained under Front control.

Rocket Artillery
At divisional level this is represented by the BM-21 122mm MLRS. The Soviets have always regarded

Left:
Soviet towed artillery is still widely used. Here, the D-20 152mm howitzer. *Author*

Above:
The earlier M1955 100mm anti-tank gun, now largely replaced by the T-12. *Novosti*

truck-borne. A new one now coming into service is the BM-27 240mm with 16 tubes, and this is going to supersede the BM-21 in time.

The other type of rocket is the heavy tactical rocket as represented at divisional level by the 'Frog-7' (known as 'Luna' by the Soviets). This has conventional, nuclear and chemical warheads. The earlier 'Frog-3' and 'Frog-4' may also still be seen, and these are mounted on tracks as opposed to the wheeled ZIL-135 on 'Frog-7'.

Surface-to-Surface Guided Missiles
The 'Scud' is found in army rocket launcher brigades. The earlier 'Scud-A' is mounted on a JS-3 chassis and is radio-guided, while 'Scud-B' is mainly found on the MAZ-543 wheeled transporter and has inertial guidance. Missiles of greater range than these are considered as strategic and are beyond the scope of this book.

Air Defence Weapons
The Soviet experience during the earlier years of the Great Patriotic War, when the Germans held air superiority over the battlefield, convinced them of the need to give their ground forces adequate

MLRS as an important supprting fire weapon, and the Germans on the Eastern Front during 1941–45 had a healthy respect for 'Stalin's Daughter'. The Czechs and East Germans also use the 122mm RM-70. Larger calibre systems, notably the BM-24 240mm, are found in Army level Rocket Launcher Brigades.

The attraction of MLRS is the simultaneous weight of concentrated fire which it can put down, with the BM-21 being able to fire 40 rounds in 30sec, but there is a drawback in the reloading time (10–15min for BM-21). All MLRS systems are

integral air defence. Consequently, air defence weapons are widely deployed at all levels, and come in two types, guns and missiles. Since fighter ground attack (FGA) and the armed helicopter are two major weapon systems in the NATO armoury for countering the armour threat, it is important that Warsaw Pact battlefield air defence assets are considered.

Guns

Within the motor rifle and tank regiments and also at army level is found the well proven radar-controlled ZSU-23-4, which is mounted on a PT-76 chassis, and is known as Shilka. The other self-propelled system is the ZSU-57-2 mounted on a T-54 chassis, but this has now been superseded in first-line units by the ZSU-23-4. The Czechs also have the M-53/59 twin 30mm cannon mounted on a Praga or Tatra truck, which is armour-plated in both cases. Towed anti-aircraft guns such as the ZPU-2 and ZPU-4 14.5mm twin and quadruple systems and the ZSU-23-2 twin 23mm have now generally been relegated to second-line units. Most AFVs also have machine guns for the air defence role.

Surface-to-Air Missiles

At the lowest level, one per platoon in the motor rifle company, is the SA-7 'Grail', an individual weapon, equivalent to the US Redeye or British Blowpipe. Recently an improved version, with greater velocity and range – the Strela-2 – has been introduced. Within the tank and motor rifle regiment is found the SA-9 'Gaskin', which is normally mounted with twin retractable launchers on BRDM-2. Both these are infra-red homing. At divisional level coverage is given by SA-6 'Gainful' or SA-8 'Gecko'. The former is mounted on a ZSU-23-4 chassis with a triple launcher, while the latter has a special 6x6 amphibious vehicle and four launchers. In support of an Army is the SA-4 'Ganef' with a specially designed tracked vehicle mounting twin launchers. SA-4, SA-6 and SA-9 use radio command guidance.

Above:
Soviet M1973 152mm SP guns. *Novosti*

Below:
The Soviets are now placing increasing emphasis on SP artillery in order to carry out the high speed offensive. Here are M1974 122mm guns deployed for firing. *Author*

Anti-Tank Weapons

Many NATO anti-armour weapons are AFV-mounted, and hence it is essential to consider what anti-armour means the Warsaw Pact deploys. These can be categorised by type (missile, gun, recoilless gun, rocket launcher) and platform (AFV, towed gun, hand-held, heliborne, aircraft).

AFV

The T-62 115mm and T-64/72 125mm tank guns are smoothbore and use three types of ammunition – APDSFS, HEATFS and HEFS with the first two being anti-armour rounds. The advantages and disadvantages of smoothbore and rifled gun barrels are covered in Chapter Two, as are the different types of attack against armour. In the airborne divisions there is a tank destroyer, ASU-85 mounting an 85mm rifled gun which fires a high velocity armoured piercing round. Also on BMP is the 73mm smoothbore gun which fires a rocket-assisted round capable of engaging tanks out to 1,000m. There are a number of anti-tank guided weapons also carried on AFVs detailed separately.

Left:
Soviet M-74 armoured fire control vehicle, which is used in conjunction with their SP artillery.
Author

Below:
'Frog-7' which can carry conventional, nuclear or chemical warheads.

Bottom:
Ideal for keeping enemy air off the back of mechanised forces, the Soviet ZSU-23-4, with its four 23mm cannon and associated radar dish.
Author

Soviet Anti-tank Guided Weapons		
		Guidance
Designation	*Range*	*System*
AT-1 'Snapper'	2,300m	Wire
AT-2 'Swatter'	2,500m	Wire
'Swatter-B'	3,000m	Infra-red seeking/radio
AT-3 'Sagger'	2,300m	Wire
'Sagger-B'	3,000m	Infra-red seeking/radio
AT-4 'Spigot'	2,000m	Infra-red seeking/wire
AT-5 'Spandrel'	2,000m	Infra-red seeking/wire

Towed Anti-Tank Guns

The anti-tank battalion of the motor rifle division is equipped with the 100mm T-12, which is a smoothbore gun using APDSFS ammunition, and will penetrate 400mm of armoured plate at the vertical at 500m range.

Recoilless Anti-Tank Guns

The 73mm SPG-9 is still found in second-line motor rifle battalions. It fires a HEAT warhead capable of penetrating 300mm of armoured plate at the vertical. However, ATGW has largely replaced this type of anti-armour weapon.

Handheld Weapons

The most well known is the RPG-7 so beloved of insurgency forces around the globe, which fires an 85mm HEAT projectile. This, however, is being replaced by the RPG-16, with 73mm warhead, with a special version for airborne troops with a launcher tube which comes in two parts. The Czechs also have the RPG P-27 with 45mm warhead.

Heliborne Weapons

The most formidable weapon here is the MI-24 'Hind' attack helicopter, and the most widespread version is the 'Hind-D', which carried a 12.7mm four-barrel Gatling gun, and either four 'Sagger' or 'Swatter' launchers or four pods each containing 32 57mm rockets. The latest version, 'Hind-E', has the tube launched 'Spiral', a second generation 'fire and forget' anti-tank missile.

Aircraft Weapons

The most common types of close support aircraft found over the battle area will be the Su-7 'Fitter', Su-17 'Fitter-D', and the more modern MiG-23 ('Flogger F and H'), MiG-27 ('Flogger D and J') and Su-24 ('Fencer'). These are equipped with 23mm Gatling cannon, and a variety of air-to-surface missiles and bombs.

Tactics

As has been previously stressed, should the Soviet Union decide to go to war in Europe, she will wish to achieve victory by conventional means alone, if possible. This means making maximum use of surprise and speed in order to achieve her military aims before NATO can come to a collective decision to retaliate with nuclear weapons. The key to her ground strategy is the art of the high speed offensive. Crucial to this is the maintenance of momentum, something which the Russians learnt to appreciate during the Great Patriotic War. The concept here is that when the first echelon has just about exhausted itself, which would mean suffering some 40% casualties or over, a fresh second echelon takes over and continues the attack. The echelon system is operated down to regimental level, but is not to be regarded as a reserve: that is comparatively small and is retained by commanders at all levels to guard against the unexpected.

Soviet planning is based on reaching the Atlantic coast in 10-14 days, and initially, until the breakthrough of the NATO defensive crust has been achieved, ground forces are expected to

Top left:
Soviet BRDMs armed with 'Swatter' ATGW are found in Motor Rifle Regiments, although nowadays first-line units will normally have BRDMs equipped with five 'Spandrel' launchers.
Novosti

Above left:
Another view of the basic T-72, this time on a parade during Exercise ZAPAD-81, a major 1981 Warsaw Pact exercise. *Novosti*

Above:
The BMD is the airportable/droppable equivalent of BMP. Note the 'Sagger' ATGW system. *Author*

Right:
The advance to contact; a Soviet T-55 platoon on the march. *Novosti*

Above:
In most respects the Soviet Mi-24 family of helicopters are the most formidable in large-scale service anywhere in the world. All models have the unusual attribute of combining attack or anti-tank weapons with a cabin for a squad of troops or other load. This is the anti-armour version called 'Hind-D' by NATO.

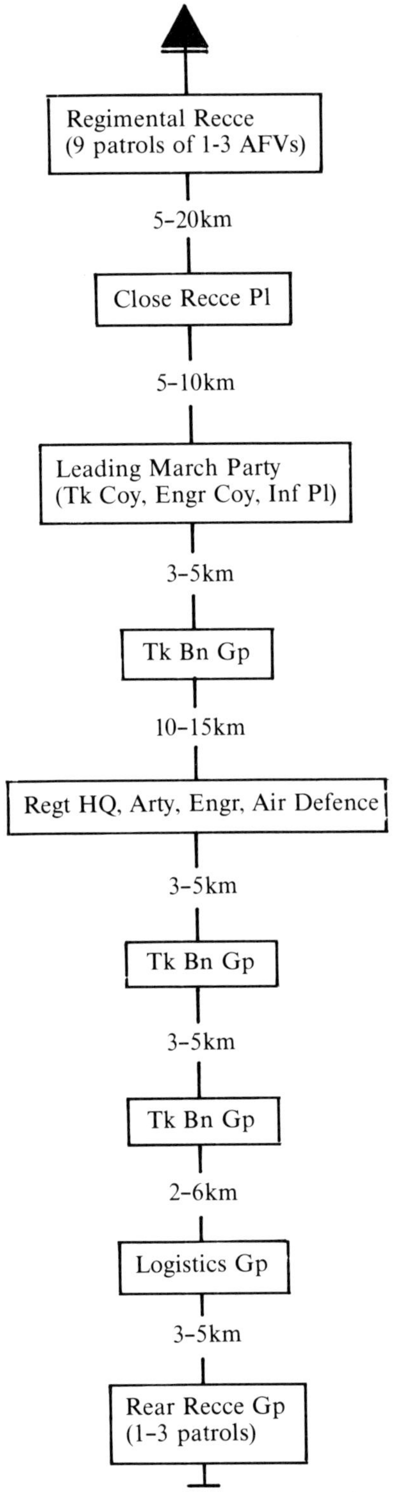

Right:
Soviet tank regiment in the advance. Because of the nuclear threat the regiment will remain dispersed until the last possible moment before making an attack.

advance 30–50km per day. In terms of frontages and depth, an army attacking on the main axis will have a frontage of some 30km, and will attack with two divisions up in the first echelon. If it is on a secondary axis, the frontage could be as much as 80km. In either case its depth will extend some 100km.

Reconnaissance
Axes of advance will have been selected well in advance, with the main criteria being terrain and prior knowledge of the initial deployment of NATO forward troops. However, there is still the need for reconnaissance, which will take many forms. While satellites and aircraft will take care of strategic reconnaissance, which is outside the scope of this book, long-range reconnaissance will be conducted by special forces' patrols, which would have been inserted prior to hostilities. Their main tasks are the location of nuclear weapons sites, headquarters and key logistic installations. As for the first echelon, aerial and signals reconnaisance will be used in conjunction with ground units. The cornerstone of the latter is the divisional reconnaissance battalion, which will operate on a frontage of 15–20km and up to a depth of 50km ahead of the main body. Army level reconnaissance elements will be inserted between divisions and on the flanks, while regimental reconnaissance companies will be used primarily for engineer and chemical observation tasks. In all

Fig 15

Regimental Recce
(9 patrols of 1-3 AFVs)

5–20km

Close Recce Pl

5–10km

Leading March Party
(Tk Coy, Engr Coy, Inf Pl)

3–5km

Tk Bn Gp

10–15km

Regt HQ, Arty, Engr, Air Defence

3–5km

Tk Bn Gp

3–5km

Tk Bn Gp

2–6km

Logistics Gp

3–5km

Rear Recce Gp
(1–3 patrols)

cases, the emphasis is on locating the main enemy positions and finding ways round them, and these units will not fight unless forced to.

The Approach March

This is a crucial part of the Soviet and Warsaw Pact operations. With the need to maintain a high rate of advance and simultaneously not sacrifice command and control, Warsaw Pact forces will not deploy tactically unless they are about to attack. Until that time they will move in 'march order'. However, an important principle is the ability of a unit to be able to deploy quickly off the line of march in order to engage the enemy, and to be aware of the nuclear threat. Therefore a division will normally move in three regimental sized increments with some 3km between each, and will probably use two routes, but not more. In order to ensure that its mobility is maintained, engineers and maintenance units will be deployed so that obstacles and disabled vehicles on the line of march can be quickly dealt with. Ahead of the main body will be the advanced guard which, in length, will be even more spread out than the main body.

The Meeting Engagement or Encounter Battle

The Soviets hope to catch NATO forces before they have deployed to battle positions, as clearly once they are firm in them more time and effort will be required to dislodge, destroy or neutralise them. Thus, if the Soviet reconnaissance elements contact the opposition while it is still on the move, the advanced guard will close up and begin engaging them. The object is then for the main body, guided by their reconnaissance, to move round and attack the enemy in the flank, thereby catching him off balance and defeating him. It must, however, be stressed that this type of operation requires great quickness and flexibility in thought and action to be successful and in this respect is more difficult for Warsaw Pact troops to carry out than their Western counterparts. Although there are signs that the Soviets are less rigid in their approach than they used to be, the initiative allowed to junior commanders is still very slender and communications are not as efficient as in the west with radios at platoon level having receivers only, but no transmitters.

The Attack

Like NATO, the Soviets have two types of attack – quick and deliberate. The former is used when the defence is considered weak, and is carried out off the line of march. Once sufficient information has been passed back by the reconnaissance elements, supporting artillery and mortars will move out to a flank to fire positions, and the three companies of the leading motor rifle battalion, which will normally be supported by a tank company, will, at about 5,000m from the enemy positions, deploy into three parallel columns. Then, at 1,000m, the APCs will deploy into line with the tanks leading and drive hard for the enemy positions, not waiting for supporting fire, which will only be used if they run into trouble and another motor rifle battalion group needs to be committed. The object of the leading units will be to break through the defences and continue the advance, leaving any

Below:
The Soviet high speed attack as used in the Great Patriotic War. Infantry riding on tanks are very vulnerable, and prevent the crew from fighting the tank. *TASS*

Left:
Nowadays, the Soviet attack is more likely to look like this. Tanks (T-62s) lead the APCs (in this case BTR-50s, with which Soviet second-line tank divisions are still equipped) onto the objective. The infantry will only dismount if the enemy resistance is strong. *Author*

mopping up to be done by follow up elements. In this way, the minimum delay is incurred. Infantry will not dismount from their vehicles if the opposition is light.

Where, however, the enemy defences are stronger, great emphasis is laid on preparatory fire, and it is worth digressing in a little detail as to how the Soviets do employ their artillery, as they regard it as crucial to success. Soviet doctrine specifies three types of fire used in support of an attack. The first is preparatory fire, which is designed to soften up the defence before the attack begins. This is followed by close support fire, which is brought down during the assault, but is not to be confused with accompanying fire, which keeps close to the attacking troops until they have broken through the defences. The main object of preparatory fire is not so much the destruction of the enemy's defences, but to demoralise the defenders so that, when the attack is launched, they are not able to man their weapons with any degree of effectiveness. It will include not just artillery fire, but rockets, mortars and fighter ground attack as well. There will be no pause after the preparatory phase. The armour and infantry will immediately begin their attack, accompanied by supporting fire, in the shape of a rolling barrage or lines of successive concentrations of fire, and accompanying fire. The tanks and MICVs will also put down suppressive fire as they move forward, the tanks generally leading. Attack helicopters will also be used to tackle troublesome strongpoints. In essense, if they have to attack well prepared positions the Soviets seek to concentrate overwhelming superiority of force against them, as much as 4–5 times in manpower and 10–15 times in weapon systems.

Units Forward of the Main Body

Apart from reconnaissance units, the Soviets also employ two other types of unit which will operate forward of the main body. Both of these, although not innovations in themselves, since they were both used in the Great Patriotic War, reflect Soviet concern over the increasing numbers of NATO anti-tank weapons to be found on the battlefield.

Forward Detachments

These are based on a reinforced motor rifle or tank unit, normally battalion sized at divisional level and found from the second echelon. The Forward Detachment will be all arms in nature with its own supporting artillery, anti-tank and engineer assets, with reconnaissance and chemical elements as well. In the advance it will move ahead to capture obstacle crossings – bridges, defiles – and will hold them until the main body joins up. In the attack, they will be used to penetrate the enemy covering forces and penetrate deep into the enemy defences to capture key positions. They are likely to operate up to some 30–50km ahead of the main body.

Operational Manoeuvre Groups (OMGs)

Although the Western Press has hailed these as a departure from the normal Soviet concept of operations, they were employed under the title of Mobile Groups on the Eastern Front, especially from 1943 onwards. They are organised on a scale of one division at army level and three at TVD level. The purpose of the OMG is to create dislocation of the enemy's defences – a traditional blitzkrieg objective – and it does this by driving deep into the enemy's territory to knock out his C^3 and logistic installations, as well as destroying his nuclear delivery means. They can also be used to disrupt enemy reserves in a meeting engagement, to establish blocking positions on the enemy's withdrawal routes and even to seize the enemy's rear defensive lines before they are occupied. In all cases, the Soviets hope to throw NATO command and control systems into confusion in that the OMG, once inserted, will force defending commanders to look in two opposing directions at once. Often it will be used in conjunction with operations by an air assault brigade. However, to be successful, it must be launched early, within 48 hours of launching a major offensive, and will aim for weak points in the enemy defence. Although it is likely to have impressive quantities of supporting fire assets, it will be at least partially dependent on main body assistance in breaking through. Furthermore, when an OMG is deployed the second echelon could well be dispensed with, and the first echelon made stronger in order to improve the chances of the OMG breaking through. Above all, the use of the OMG depends on surprise and if the enemy has had sufficient time to set up a coherent and strong defence it is unlikely to be employed.

Defence of the Central Region

The Central Region of Europe, in NATO terms, is defined as the whole of the Federal Republic of Germany less the Schleswig-Holstein peninsula in the north, and makes up one of the three major NATO commands in Europe. Under the overall charge of Supreme Allied Commander Europe (SACEUR), with his headquarters at Mons in Belgium, these three commands are: Northern Europe, which covers Norway, Denmark and Schleswig-Holstein; Southern Europe (Italy, Greece and Turkey, as well as Portugal and Spain); and Central Europe. Commander-in-Chief Central Europe, with his headquarters at Brunssum

Below:
US M1 Abrams. First production models mount the British 105mm rifled gun as used on M60, but this is now being replaced by Rheinmetall's 120mm smoothbore, which is mounted on Leopard 2. *General Dynamics Land Systems Division*

in the Netherlands, controls two army groups, Northern and Central.

Northern Army Group (NORTHAG) is traditionally commanded by a British officer, who also doubles as Commander-in-Chief British Army of the Rhine (BAOR) and has his headquarters at Reindahlen, near Mönchen-Gladbach on the edge of the Ruhr. Under him he has four national corps – Belgian, British, Dutch and German – and these defend a line along the Inner German Border (IGB) from the Baltic down to Kassel. Central Army Group (CENTAG) covers the area south of this down to the Austrian border and this represents some 60% of the Central Region frontage. From his headquarters at Heidelberg, its US commander controls two American and two German corps. It also has an independent Canadian brigade. Collocated with both HQ NORTHAG and HQ CENTAG are two Allied air forces – 2nd Allied Tactical Air Force (ATAF) and 4 ATAF respectively.

Originally, when NATO forces were first organ-

ised in the early 1950s, the concept was to fight a delaying battle back towards the Rhine and then hold there. After the Federal Republic of Germany was granted NATO membership in the mid-1950s, the main defensive line was moved forward. However, it must be emphasised that up until 1967, in view of the marked Warsaw Pact conventional superiority but nuclear inferiority, NATO defence of the Central Region rested on the doctrine of 'massive retaliation', which meant that any Warsaw Pact incursion of West Germany would be met with an all out nuclear attack. Then, in view of growing Soviet nuclear capability, the doctrine of 'flexible response' was adopted. This envisaged forces balanced between conventional and nuclear, capable of reacting to a range of crises without necessarily having to resort to nuclear war. At the same time the Germans, recognising that hostilities in Germany were now likely to go through a conventional phase, demanded that NATO forces must be prepared to defend the whole of the Federal Republic and that it was politically unacceptable voluntarily to surrender the most easterly belt of the country. Out of this was borne

the Forward Defence concept, which is still current today. NATO forces must make every effort to defend in place from the moment that the enemy crosses the IGB, and only to give ground when they are forced to do so.

The threat, as perceived by NATO forces in the Central Region, could be as large as 101 Warsaw Pact divisions directed against Central Europe, of which the vast majority are facing the Central Region. Currently stationed in East Germany, Czechoslovakia and Poland are 58 divisions, with 19,000 MBTs, and a further 33 divisions, with 8,500

Below:
M1 Abrams being put through its paces. The commander has a 12.7mm and the loader a 7.62mm machine gun, both primarily for air defence. A further 7.62mm is mounted coaxially with the main armament. *General Dynamics Land Systems Division*

Right:
These Danish infantrymen are using their Carl Gustavs somewhat suicidally against British Chieftains. *Armed Forces*

tanks, can be deployed in a matter of days from the Baltic, Belorussian, and Carpathian Military Districts, Ten Warsaw Pact divisions (2,700 tanks) stationed in Hungary could also be used in the Central Region, although their prime role is in Southern Europe.

To face this threat, NATO is heavily reliant on 28 divisions and 6,500 MBTs already stationed in the Federal Republic, and in considering the anti-armour battle it is these formations which will be examined although, in time of imminent danger, considerable reinforcements will begin to deploy, especially from the United States under the 'Reforger' programme, and the likelihood that the French, although not militarily part of NATO, would, if the Warsaw Pact crossed the IGB, commit its sizeable forces to the Alliance. Because no less than six nations are currently actively involved in the defence of the Central Region, and unit organisations for each vary, it is proposed to concentrate primarily on the Germans and Americans, who make the largest contribution, and to merely point out where major differences lie in the organisations of other armies.

The two army groups involved each control four corps. NORTHAG, looking from north to south in terms of deployment in the field, is made up as follows:

1 (NL) Corps
1st Division (three armoured infantry brigades), 4th Division (two armoured and one armoured infantry brigade), which are both stationed in Germany, a reserve division in the Netherlands,

5th Division (one armoured and two armoured infantry brigades) and a reserve brigade, 101st Brigade.

1 (GE) Corps
1st Panzer Grenadier (Pz Gren) Division, 11th Pz Gren Division (each two armoured infantry and one tank brigades) 3rd Panzer Division (two tank and one armoured infantry brigade).

1 (BR) Corps
1st and 4th Armoured Divisions (each three armoured brigades), 3rd Armoured Division (two armoured brigades – one of which has been con-verted into a trial airmobile brigade – and one infantry brigade, which would come from UK), 2nd Infantry Division (three infantry brigades all UK based).

1 (BE) Corps
1st Division (three mechanised brigades, one of which is a reserve brigade based in Belgium) 16th Division (one armoured brigade, two mechanised brigades, one of which is based in Belgium).

In addition, Commander NORTHAG (COMNORTHAG) has the German 7th Panzer Division as his reserve. He thus has a total of 13 divisions, of which eight are complete in Germany, three are partially complete and two, 3rd (UK) and 3rd (NL) Divisions, have to be deployed from its national territory.

CENTAG, again looking from north to south, is organised as follows:

III (GE) Corps

2nd Panzer Grenadier Division (two armoured infantry and one tank brigades), 5th Panzer Division (two tank and one armoured brigades), and Luftlande Brigade 26 (airborne).

Below:
A Chieftain passing a Milan ATGW position. The gun barrel is camouflaged to break up its outline.
Armed Forces

Bottom:
Chieftain is being partially replaced by Challenger in the British Army of the Rhine (BAOR). It retains the 120mm rifled gun. Note the similar turret shape to M1 Abrams.
Royal Ordnance Factories

V (US) Corps

8th Mechanised Infantry Division (three brigade HQs with four tank and six mechanised infantry battalions), 3rd Armored Division (three brigade HQs with six tank and four mechanised infantry battalions), 4th Brigade of 4th Mechanised Division (remainder of division in CONUS), and 11th Armoured Cavalry Regiment.

VII (US) Corps

12th (GE) Panzer Division (two tank and one armoured infantry brigades) 3rd Mechanised Infantry Division (three brigade HQs with four tank and six mechanised infantry battalions), 1st Armored Division (three brigade HQs with six tank and four mechanised infantry battalions), 3rd

Brigade of the 1st Mechanised Infantry Division (remainder in CONUS, but will be deployed under 'Reforger'); the 2nd and 3rd Armoured Cavalry Regiments would also be flown across under 'Reforger'.

II (GE) Corps
4th Panzer Grenadier Division (two armoured infantry and one tank brigades), 10th Panzer

Below:
The US Armor Battalion

Bottom:
The US Mechanised Battalion.

Division (two tank and one armoured infantry brigades) 1st Gebirge (Mountain) Division (one armoured infantry brigade, one tank brigade, one mountain infantry brigade), Luftlande Brigade 25 and HQ9 Luftlande Division.

COMCENTAG'S immediate reserve is the 4th Canadian Mechanised Brigade Group (CMBG). In addition, both NORTHAG and CENTAG are supported by the German Territorial Command, specifically German Territorial Northern Command (GTNC) with headquarters at Mönchen Gladbach and German Territorial Southern Command (GTSC) with its headquarters also close by that of CENTAG at Heidelberg. These consist of a number of brigades, including some

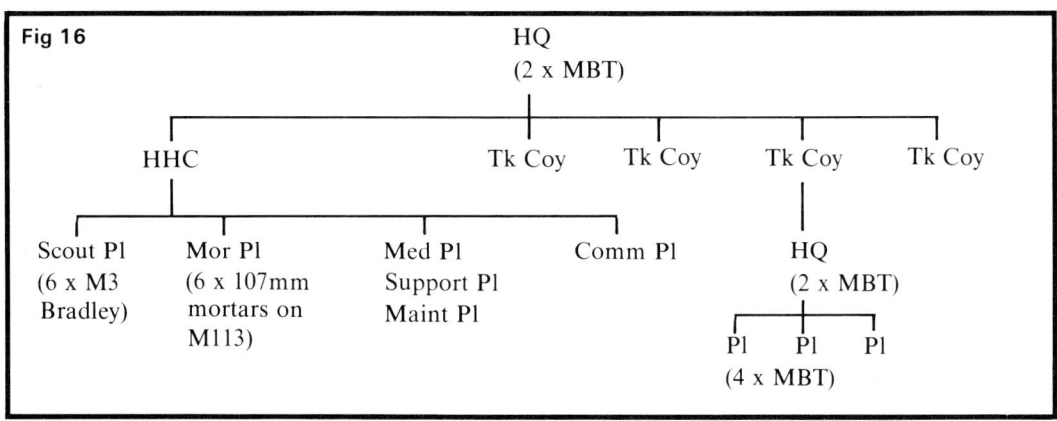

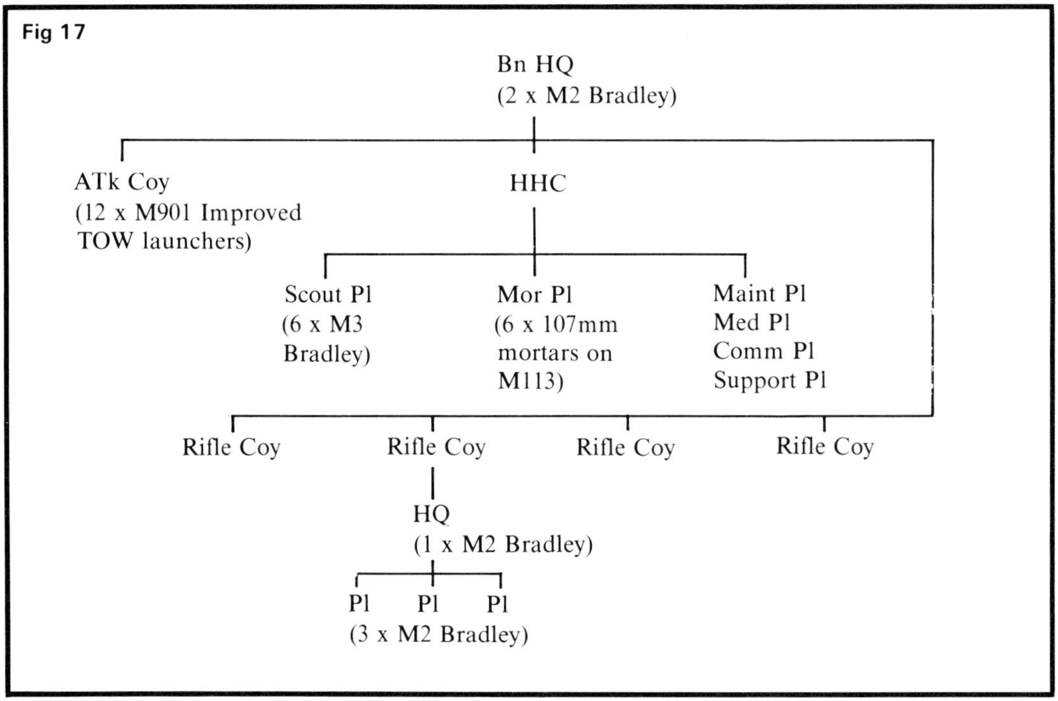

Above:
A Challenger negotiates a German village.
HQ 1 Armd Div PR

Right:
Leopard 1 has now been mainly relegated to the German Territorial Forces, but is still used by the Belgians, Canadians and Dutch in the NATO Central Region. It mounts the British 105mm rifled gun. *Author*

armour, and will be responsible for rear area security.

It will be noted that there are a number of different types of division within the national contributions to the Central Region. However, most attention will be concentrated on the two main types – armoured and mechanised infantry.

The US Division
The Americans, unlike their allies, do not have fixed organisations for their brigades, merely a laid down number of armoured and mechanised infantry battalions in each type of division. Thus, each of the three brigade HQs within the division will be allocated a number of battalions for a particular operation depending on the divisional commander's appreciation of the situation. This concept originated with the armoured divisions of World War 2, which each had a number of combat commands, again *ad hoc* formations. The only other nation to experiment with this was the British, who used it, with what they called Task Force HQs in the latter half of the 1970s, but have now reverted back to the traditional fixed brigade

system. Thus, given that each armoured division has six armoured and five mechanised infantry battalions, and each mechanised division six mechanised infantry and four infantry battalions, it is simpler to examine first the organisation of the two types of battalion and then go on to consider the supporting arms present in the division.

At this present time the US division in Europe is undergoing a reorganisation to reflect both the introduction of the M1 Abrams MBT and M2/3 Bradley MICV as well as the new American doctrine 'AirLand Battle', of which more later. This new division, known as Division 86, is the main tool with which the US Army in Europe will defend the Central Region in the future and hence this will be covered in detail rather than the existing organisation, which can now be considered as obsolescent. However, major differences between the new and old establishments will be highlighted.

The Armor Battalion
The present organisation consists of 54 M60 series MBTs, divided into three companies each of three

platoons of five tanks each, with two in company headquarters and a further three at battalion HQ. The new battalion will have 58 M1 Abrams or M60A3s, with two at battalion HQ and four tank companies, each of three platoons of four tanks each. Furthermore the scout (reconnaissance) platoon will see its M113s superseded by six M3 Bradleys, and the combat support company, which used to control the scout, mortar, armoured vehicle launched bridge (AVLB) and Redeye SAM platoons, has now been eradicated. While both

Above:
A Dutch Leopard 2 *Author*

Below:
Leopard 2 armed with the Rheinmetall 120mm smoothbore gun. *Krauss-Maffei*

Redeye and AVLB platoons have been dropped, the remaining two platoons have been put under the head and headquarters company (HHC), which also now controls all supply assets,

'chopping' off slices to each tank company as the situation warrants. This includes repair resources, which used to be integral to each company. The new armour battalion organisation is shown diagrammatically at Fig 16.

The Mechanised Battalion
This follows a similar pattern of reorganisation. Here again the three rifle companies of the existing organisation have been increased to four, and the combat support company has been merged into HHC. An anti-tank company has also been formed, and HHC chops a maintenance slice to each company. See Fig 17.

The Divisional Base
This is common to both types of division, and consists of command and control, reconnaissance, combat support and administrative support elements.

Above:
The Germans and Belgians use the KJPZ4-5 tank destroyer, which has an effective range of 1500m. They are organised in brigade anti-tank companies. *Bundesministerium der Verteidigung*

Below:
Although now virtually obsolete in NATO armies, the Danes still have some British Centurions.
HQ UKLF PR

Right:
HOT missile launchers can be mounted on a variety of AFVs. This quadruple launcher is on the British MCV-80. *GKN Sankey*

Below right:
A US M88 armoured recovery vehicle.
HQ BAOR PR

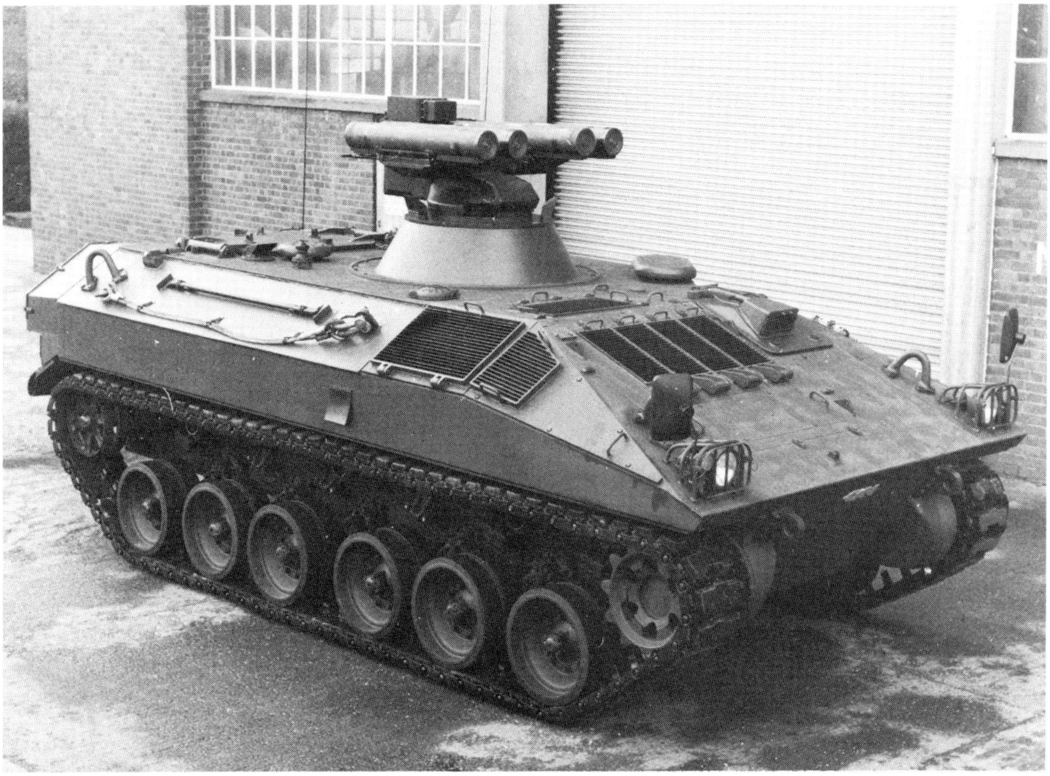

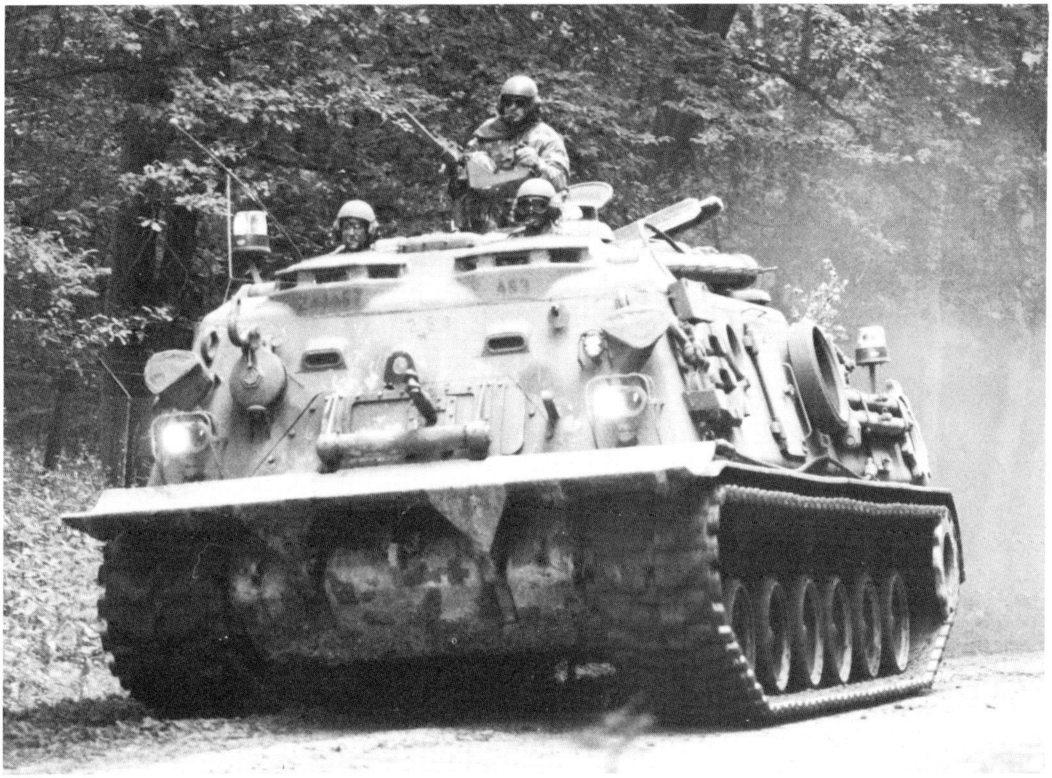

Left:
The Chieftain bridgelayer can span a gap of 24m. It is a very useful aid to armour mobility. *Armed Forces*

Below:
US M551 Sheridan. This mounts a 152mm gun/missile launcher, firing the Shillelagh missile and HEAT. Originally conceived as a reconnaissance vehicle it has now been largely replaced by the M3 Bradley. *US Armor & Engineer Board*

Right:
Scorpion, the main reconnaissance vehicle used by the British and Belgians. Its 76mm gun is very effective against light armoured vehicles, and its aluminium armour gives it a very low nominal ground pressure, enabling it to traverse soft ground. *Author*

Below right:
Scimitar, with the 30mm Rarden cannon, with its 'burst fire' capability, is often used with Scorpion in the reconnaissance role. *Author*

Field Artillery Three battalions of M109 155mm self-propelled howitzers, each of 18 guns broken down into three six-gun batteries, and one M110 203mm (8in) SP howitzer battalion with three four-gun batteries.

Air Defense Artillery Currently one battalion of two Vulcan batteries (12 weapon systems each) and two Chaparral SAM batteries (12 systems per battery). Vulcan is being replaced by the Sgt York twin 40mm gun system with 36 being deployed to the battalion.

Multiple Launch Rockets One battery of nine MLRS systems.

Armoured Cavalry Squadron This provides the division's reconnaissance assets, and consists of two armoured cavalry troops and two air cavalry troops. The armoured cavalry troop is made up of three platoons each of six Bradley M3s, with one more at Squadron headquarters, and three 107mm mortar carriers. The air cavalry troop has six scout and four attack helicopters. The squadron also has a motorcycle platoon and an NBC platoon with nine reconnaissance vehicles.

Aviation Company This provides the commander with command, control and liaison assets and has six observation and four utility helicopters. Each brigade HQ also has a further four observation helicopters, and the divisional artillery a further nine, together with two utility helicopters.

Engineer Battalion Four combat engineer

companies, each including two combat engineer vehicles (CEV) with 165mm petards, and a bridging company with Class 60 or mobile assault bridging and six AVLBs.

Signals Battalion

Military Police Company

Divisional Support Command (DISCOM) Includes medical, supply and transport, and maintenance battalions.

Other NATO Divisions

All other NATO formations within the Central Region use the brigade as a fixed formation rather than as merely a headquarters capable of commanding a flexible number of manoeuvre batta-

lions. Like the Americans, the Germans are also in the midst of a reorganisation which is designed to slim down their tank and mechanised infantry battalions, but to provide more of them; in future there will be four rather than the current three per brigade. The tank battalion will now have 41 Leopard 2s instead of the present 54, and there will be three battalions in each panzer brigade. One of these will, however, be mixed with 28 tanks and 11 MICVs, and the panzer brigade will also have a panzer grenadier battalion with 35 MICVs. The panzer grenadier brigade will now have one tank battalion, two panzer grenadier battalions each of 34 MICVs and a mixed battalion of 24 MICVs and 13 tanks. In addition, each brigade has its own

Above:
The British Ferret scout car, although largely replaced by Fox in the reconnaissance role, is still used as a liaison vehicle. *Author*

Left:
Fox, which is also armed with the 30mm Rarden. It will usually operate within 1 (BR) Corps in the rear area security role. *Ministry of Defence*

Below left:
The German Luchs reconnaissance vehicle. Although it has very good mobility, some observers consider it too large for the role, especially in view of its comparatively light armament (20mm cannon). *Author*

Above right:
US M113½ Lynx, here seen in typical Central Region terrain, is used by the Dutch and, until recently, the Canadians as a reconnaissance vehicle. *Author*

Right:
The Canadians have recently begun to produce the Swiss Mowag Piranha series of light armoured vehicles under licence. This is the Cougar fire support vehicle using the British Scorpion turret. *Diesel Division, General Motors of Canada Ltd*

155mm SP howitzer supporting artillery battalion with 18 guns, reconnaissance platoon, tank distribution company, armoured engineer company, maintenance and supply companies.

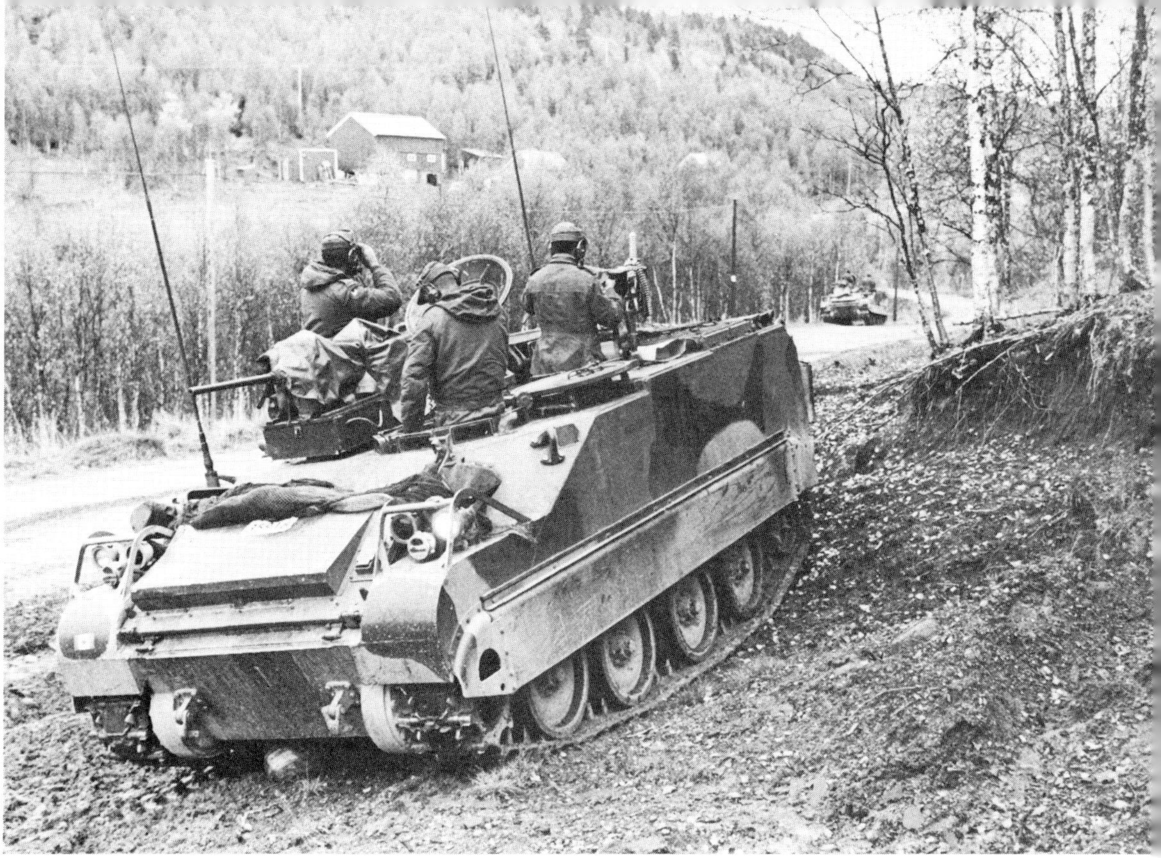

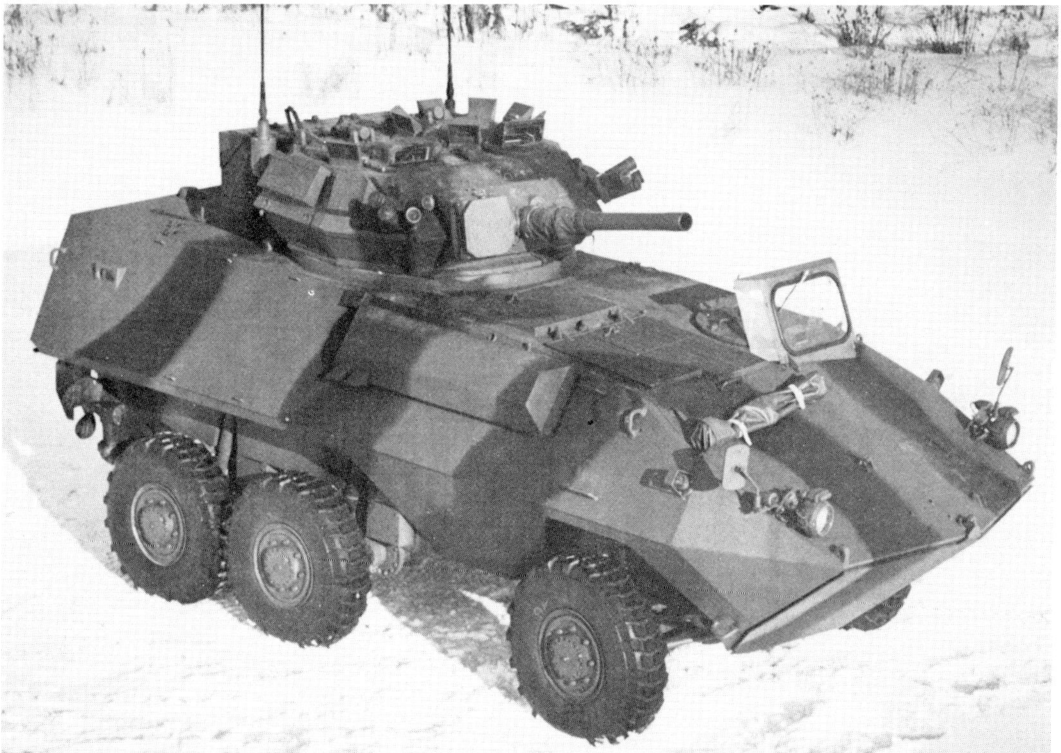

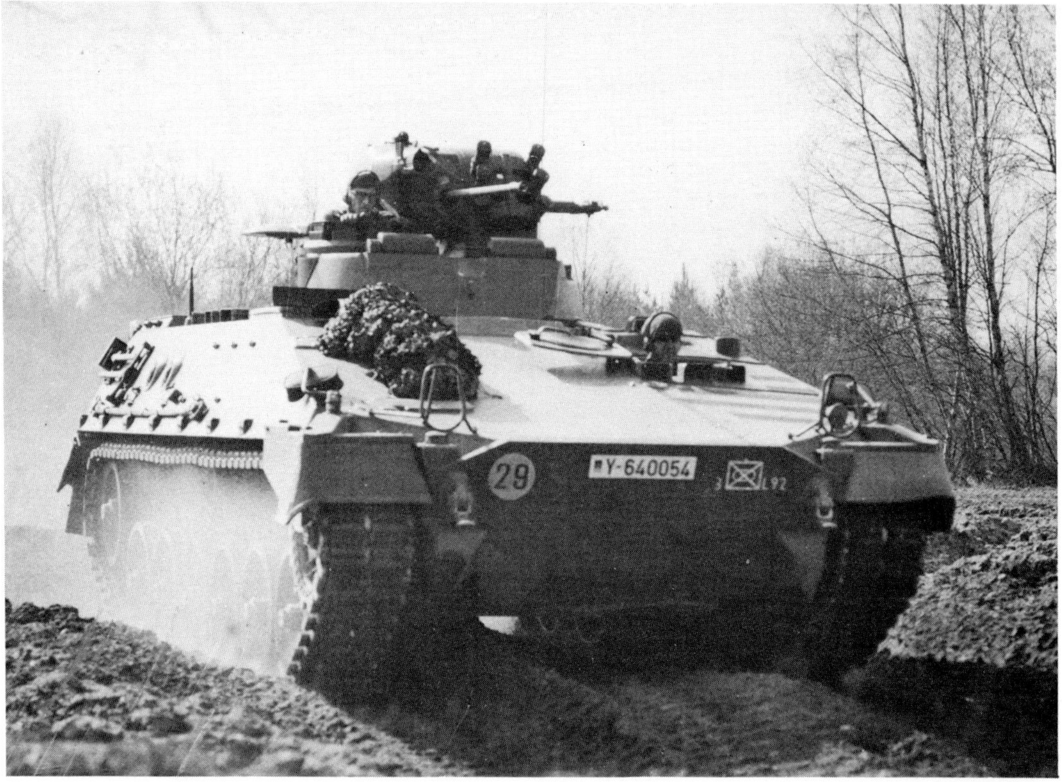
29
Y-640054

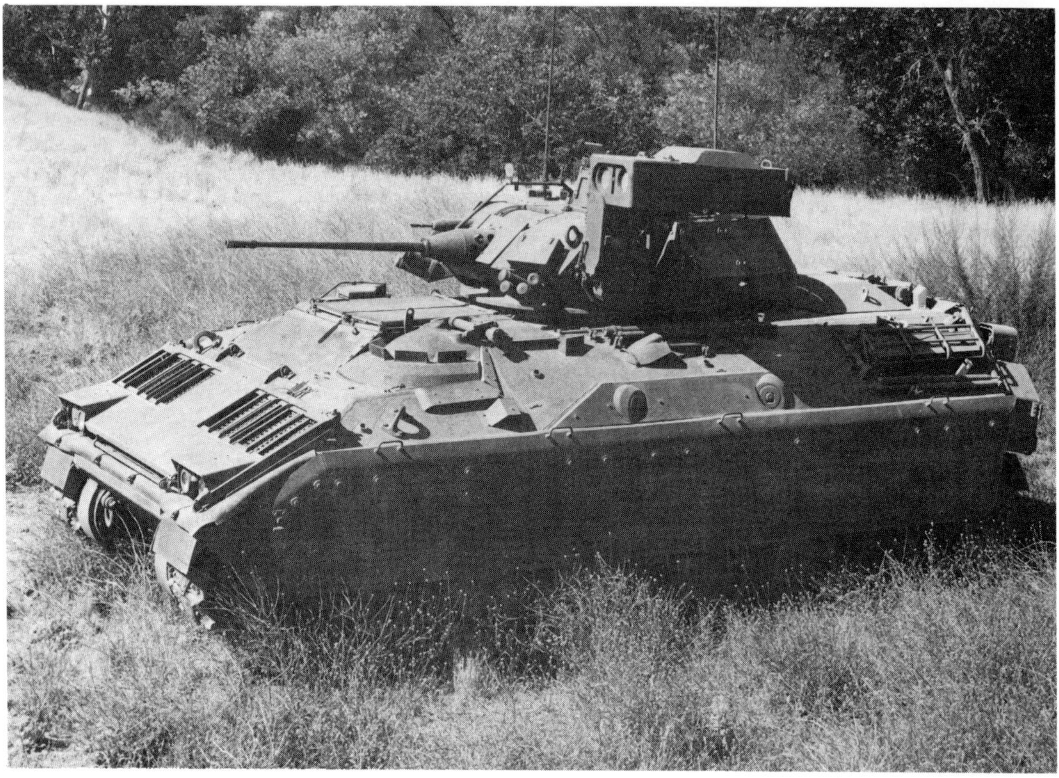

Above left:
Federal Republic of Germany Marder with its 20mm cannon. Six infantrymen are carried in the back. *Author*

Left:
M2/3 Bradley. The Cavalry fighting version has a 5-man crew including two observers, and carries additional TOW missiles. *FMC Corporation*

Above:
M2/3 Bradley, with a good view of the twin TOW launcher on the lefthand side of the turret. The Infantry Fighting Vehicle (M2) has a driver, commander and gunner and carries seven infantrymen. *FMC Corporation*

Below:
MCV-80 with the 30mm Rarden gun, which is about to enter British Army service. *GKN Sankey*

The British do not differentiate between armoured and mechanised infantry brigades, and in general these are organised as triangular brigades with two armoured regiments (equivalent to US battalion) and one mechanised infantry battalion. Some brigades, however, have one armoured regiment and two mechanised infantry battalions. The infantry brigades are not mechanised, and each has three infantry battalions, which are partially motorised. (The mobility of UK-based regular infantry battalions is now being enchanced by the issue of Saxon APCs.) The armoured regiment has 57 MBTs, which can increase in war and is divided into four squadrons, and has one reconnaissance and one ATGW troop (US platoons). The latter had been made the responsibility of the Royal Artillery in the mid-1970s, with an anti-tank battery under divisional control, but the Royal Armoured Corps has now reassumed responsibility. The mechanised infantry battalion is organised on very similar lines to its US counterpart.

The Belgians have a somewhat similar brigade organisation, with two mechanised and one tank battalion in their mechanised brigades, although the armoured brigade does have an additional tank battalion. Each brigade also has a 105mm SP howitzer battalion, and an anti-tank company with TOW ATGW. The Dutch brigades are

Above:
**The ubiquitous US M113 APC, still in use in
many countries and much seen around the NATO
Central Region. Several different variants exist,
but in its basic configuration it can carry up to 11
infantrymen.** *US Army*

Right:
**Another view of M113, this time in Dutch Army
service and its washboard down ready for
swimming.** *Author*

organised on very similar lines. Both the Belgians
and the Dutch have also made their divisional
headquarters into strictly operational command
cells, with all logistic responsibilities being undertaken by the corps headquarters, which deals
direct with brigades. The corps will also allocate
additional artillery, engineer and aviation assets to
the divisions. The German and British divisions,
on the other hand, like the American, are capable
of operating independently for limited periods,
having their own logistic resources. However, they
do differ in that the German division has its own
integral reconnaissance battalion, while British
medium range reconnaissance assets are initially
controlled by the corps, as are the Belgian, which is
out of step with the other national corps. Furthermore, the British also control close support
artillery at divisional level, although normally
each brigade can expect to receive one 24 gun
regiment in direct support. One other significant
difference at divisional level is that none of the
other national corps can boast of anything like the
US division's helicopter assets.

At corps level are held additional artillery,

engineer and aviation assets. In the case of the first of these, this is normally nuclear artillery and counter-battery, as well as locating units. The British, Belgians and Americans (through their armoured cavalry regiment) retain significant reconnaissance elements at corps in order to fight what is known as the covering force battle. The Germans, too, have corps tank regiments, which under their reorganisation, are being converted into brigades, each of three battalions of 33 tanks each, which will normally be detached to under divisional command.

One final point is that it is general NATO policy to mix infantry and armour at battalion and company level. The US Task Force, or British

Above left:
Britain's FV432, which, in spite of the introduction of MCV-80, is likely to remain in service for many years to come. Up to 10 infantrymen can be carried. *MOD (PR)*

Left:
AT-105 Saxon wheeled APC with which UK based Regular infantry battalions with a reinforcement role to BAOR are now being equipped. It was originally designed as an internal security vehicle. *GKN Sankey*

Below:
Another wheeled APC is the Dutch YP-408, although it has now been largely replaced by the XM765, an early contender for the US Army's MICV. *Author*

Battle Group, is based on a battalion head-quarters, and will consist of a number of armour and infantry companies, while at company level combat teams are formed with a mix of platoons. These are altered as dictated by the tactical situation.

NATO Tactical Doctrine

Within the framework of forward defence, the doctrines of the national corps do vary. The Germans, understandably, follow the concept most literally, and seek, if possible, to destroy the

Above:
West German Marders led by a Leopard 2 redeploy. *Bundesministerium der Verteidigung*

Below:
Another view of Marder in action. *Armed Forces*

Above right:
British FV432 APCs in the attack. This version has a turret mounted 7.62mm machine gun. *Armed Forces*

Right:
A NATO equivalent to the ZSU 23-4, the German Gepard with its twin 35mm guns. *Author*

enemy very close to the IGB. The British and Americans, as well as the Dutch and Belgians, place their main defensive position on a suitable natural obstacle, which may be at a distance from the IGB. Indeed, the Americans, with their 'AirLand Battle' concept, are now wanting to fight a much more fluid battle, using high speed manoeuvre rather than static defences as the bedrock. This, however, would mean changing NATO's overall concept of defence in the Central Region, and has yet to be accepted by the Alliance as a whole.

As it is, NATO plans to fight the battle in three phases – the covering force battle, the main defensive battle, counter-attack.

The Covering Force Battle
This is conducted by reconnaissance elements, supported by artillery and fixed and rotary wing aircraft, and sometimes reinforced by armour and mechanised infantry. Each national corps fights its own battle, but will naturally tie in as closely as it can to its neighbours. The covering forces have three main tasks. Firstly, they will attempt to identify the enemy's main axes of advance, while,

Above:
The British Rapier surface-to-air missile system, here in its towed configuration. Tracked Rapier, now coming into service, will be very much quicker to deploy. *Ministry of Defence*

Below:
The US M163 Vulcan air defence system incorporating a 20mm Gatling gun. It will be replaced in time by the Sgt York twin 40mm gun system. *Author*

at the same time, his reconnaissance elements are destroyed. They will also try to buy time so that the main defensive position can be more firmly established.

The Main Position
This is normally based on a river or canal, and even the Germans will prepare such a position, and then deploy further forward, with the object of ₃rying to defeat the enemy before he reaches it. The defence is built around the anti-armour weapons with infantry dug in. Depth brigades will have what are called counter-penetration tasks, moving to pre-planned positions in order to block enemy breakthroughs.

The Counter-Attack
Strong armour heavy reserves are held back in order to counter-attack the enemy should he break through the main position. These are held at both corps and army group level. This is seen as the decisive phase, and is aimed at halting the enemy's drive by catching him in the flank off balance, and then driving him back over the Border. If it fails to halt him, the likelihood is that NATO will be forced to resort to the use of tactical nuclear weapons.

Basic Tank Tactics

Before considering the anti-armour battle in the Central Region in its widest context, it is necessary to have an understanding of basic tank tactics. The prime roles of the tank are anti-armour and infantry support, as well as 'shock action', which is reflected in the attack and counter-attack. In spite of the multitude of threats to it, armour, if intelligently handled, can still be decisive on the battlefield. There are, however, a number of basic tactical rules born of hard experience, which tank elements must observe if they are to survive.

'One Tank is No Tank'
A tank operating on its own is very vulnerable.

Right:
M1 Abrams moving up, somewhere in Germany. The ever constant air threat means that AFVs must keep a distance from one another in order not to present too tempting a target.
HQ USAREUR

Below:
When moving across open ground, tanks, as this Chieftain shows, always move at top speed, covered by other tanks in static positions.
Armed Forces

Hence tanks never move when contact with the enemy is likely unless covered by observation and fire from other tanks. Within NATO, the basic sub-unit, the four-tank platoon or troop, will normally split into two two-tank sections for movement. While one section moves the other tanks take up fire positions from which they can cover the ground over which the other section is moving. The latter will then halt and cover the former. This is known as movement by 'bounds'. The Soviets observe this rule in a slightly different form in that

Right:
Tank Positions.
(a) Turret down – for observing. From front only radio aerial and commander's sight and MG can be seen.
(b) Hull down – for firing. From front complete turret can be seen.
(c) Tracks up – this should be for manoeuvre only. From front entire tank can be seen.

Below:
NATO armour will remain in hides until the enemy is close. The German beech wood, in which this Chieftain has sought cover, is ideal for armour. *Soldier*

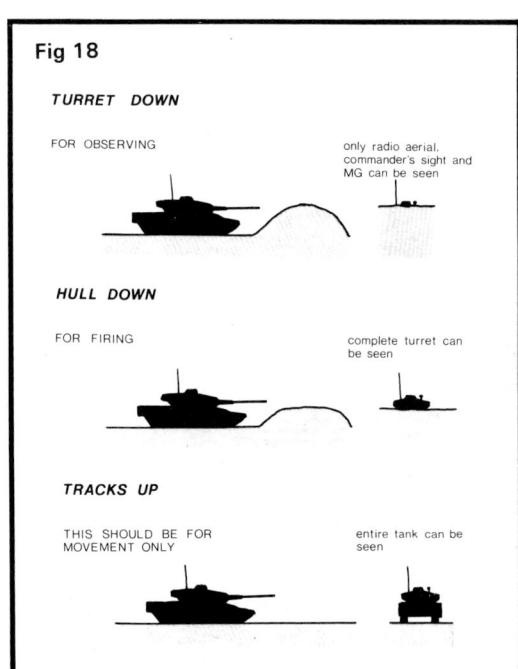

Fig 18

TURRET DOWN

FOR OBSERVING

only radio aerial, commander's sight and MG can be seen

HULL DOWN

FOR FIRING

complete turret can be seen

TRACKS UP

THIS SHOULD BE FOR MOVEMENT ONLY

entire tank can be seen

Left:
M1 Abrams advancing at speed. The stabiliser
enables the main armament and coaxial machine
gun to be fired accurately on the move.
SHAPE

Above:
'Bombing up' a Dutch Leopard 1. An APDS round
is being loaded. Note the smoke grenade
dischargers, for local protection by smoke, just
above the pistol port. *Armed Forces*

for reasons of command and control they do not
split the tank platoon.

Minimum Exposure

Because the tank is a relatively large target, it is
vital for its self preservation that it is exposed to
possible enemy observation and fire for the
shortest possible time. During tactical movement
it will always motor at best possible speed. Like-
wise, when engaging the enemy from a fire position
it will never remain in precisely the same place for
more than one or two rounds. Instead, it will use a
number of alternative fire positions, engaging a
target from one, then reversing back behind cover
and coming up in a different place before taking
on the next target. This will minimise the chances
of the enemy spotting it from the flash of its gun
and destroying it. By the same token, because of
the threat of observation from the air, tanks will
never deploy to their fire positions until the enemy

approach is imminent, remaining hidden in woods,
or possibly villages, in what are called 'hides'. The
tank which is caught in the open can use one of two
methods to prevent being hit. All tanks now have
smoke grenade dischargers mounted on either
side of the turret, and these are fired electrically
from inside. The local smokescreen produced is
sufficient to cover the tank from observation in the
frontal arc. For Western tanks this is normally of
the order of 140°, but somewhat narrower for
Soviet tanks. The other option is to fire while on
the move with the object of obscuring the enemy
gunner's line of sight. Soviet tanks, when
attacking, fire as they move as a standard tactic,
aiming to keep the defenders' heads down so that
they cannot fire back. NATO tanks, on the other
hand, tend to use machine gun fire only when
giving mobile support to attacking infantry. All
modern tanks have gun stabiliser systems to
enable them to fire accurately on the move.

Awareness of the Limitations of Armour

Although tanks and other AFVs are, by virtue of their tracks or multi-wheel drive, designed for cross-country movement, they are still limited by terrain. Soft or boggy ground can severely restrict movement. Wooded and hilly country and built-up areas, which dominate much of the Central Region, also provide problems. Water obstacles, both natural and man-made also restrict the mobility of armour. Operating in this type of close country produces not just problems of traffic-ability, but also the threat of AFV ambushes by infantry on their feet. When armour has to operate in this environment, which it will inevitably have to in Western Europe, it will be very dependent on infantry to flush out ambush parties. If obstacles, such as ditches and barriers are encountered, then it will be a question of using combat engineers, with their specialist equipment, to clear them. There is another side to the coin, however. Good tank country is that which is open and has firm going, but here the AFV is vulnerable to the long range anti-tank weapon, ATGW, the tank gun and the combat aircraft.

Visibility from inside the AFV is another limita-tion. Although AFVs are equipped with sufficient devices to give crews 360° vision, the field of view is

Above:
Infantry dismount from a Saxon APC. Note the commander giving covering fire. *HQ BAOR PR*

Above right:
The interior of a typical APC – the British Army Saxon. It can carry eight infantrymen. *GKN Sankey*

Right:
A cheap way to convert an APC into a MICV is by the addition of a suitable turret. Here is an M113 mounting a 25mm Oerlikon. *Oerlikon Military Products Division*

still restricted when compared with being outside the tank. There is a school of thought which believes that this will force tank commanders to go into action with their heads out of the turret in order to overcome this problem. Certainly the Israelis have always done this, but the penalty is a high incidence of casualties to commanders. This was their experience in the 1973 Yom Kippur War. The likelihood of having to operate in a chemical and/or nuclear environment in the Central Region, apart from the numerous threats from conven-tional weapons, will force commanders to remain closed down. Again, the problem is more severe in closer country. By night, in spite of night viewing aids, the AFV can also be very vulnerable. When closed down, the crew surrender their ability to hear, which is more important than vision for detecting enemy movement at night. This also makes AFVs vulnerable to tank hunting parties and means that either they must seek local protection by infantry or find sentries from among their own crews.

A further problem is the need for replenishment. High fuel consumption and limited ammunition stowage capacity mean that when in action the tank needs to be replenished once every 24 hours. Because of the air threat this almost invariably takes place at night and is ideally carried out when the tanks are moving to a new position – what is

called a 'running' replenishment – or, slightly less satisfactory in terms of security and speed of replenishment, in a hide. The worst possible situation is when tanks are forced to replenish in the middle of a battle. Here it is often the case of withdrawing a tank at a time from its fire position, with the danger by night that this will be given away because of the noise of the tank engine.

AFV Radio Communications
More than anything else, it is the radio communications installed in an AFV which give it its flexibility. The facility to pass information quickly and to issue fresh verbal orders in response to rapidly changing situations is most important in the quick moving armoured battle. Therefore, every armoured vehicle is equipped with radio sets. There are three types used:

Very High Frequency (VHF) This operates on frequencies between 30 and 300MHz. VHF make up the majority of ground combat radios. VHF radio waves operate on the line of sight principle and this limits the radio range, which is normally not more than 20–25km in typical Central Region terrain.
High Frequency (HF) The frequency range is 3–30MHz. HF operates on surface waves, which gives increased range over VHF, but is more difficult to operate because of the background clutter, which becomes particularly bad at night. It

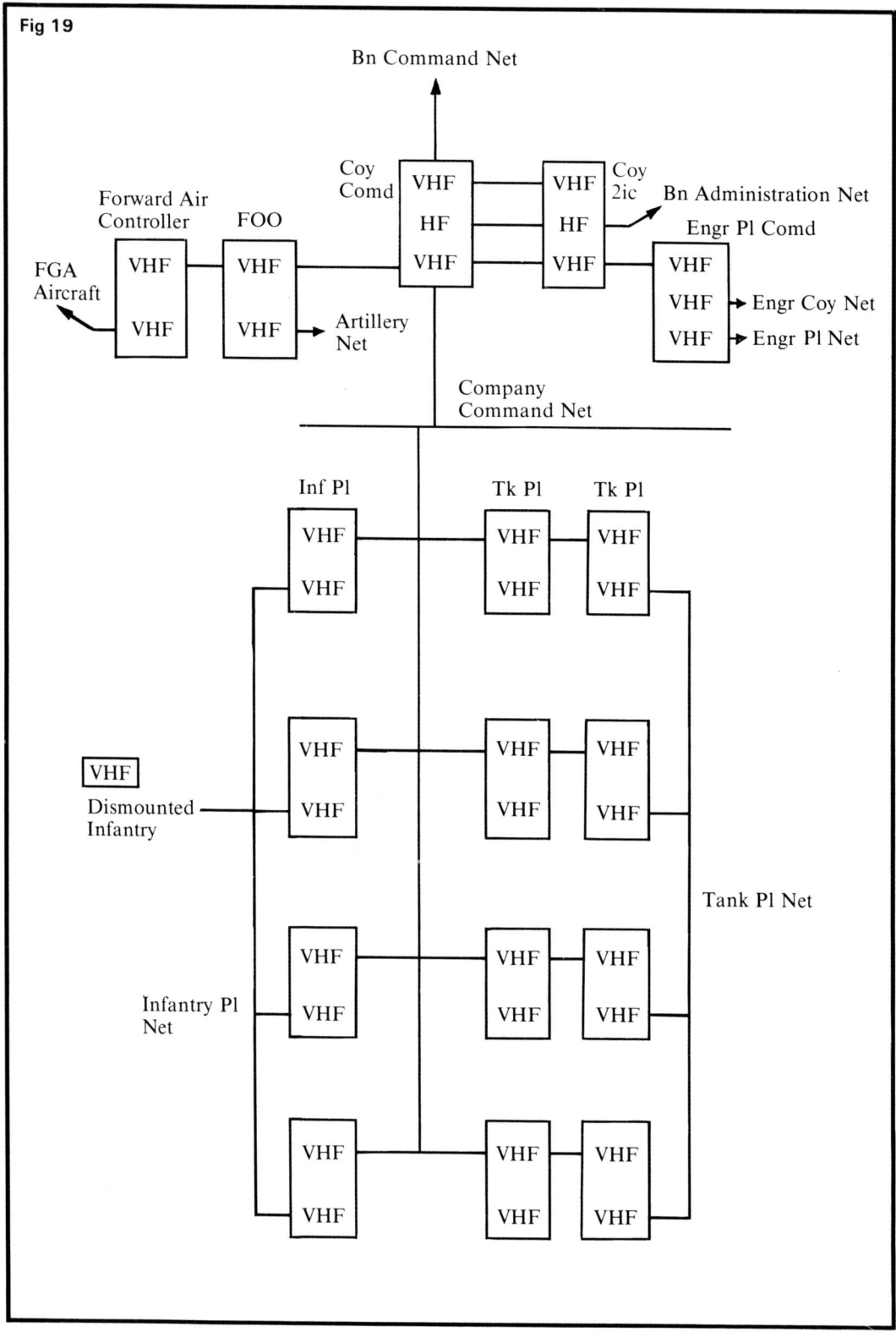

Fig 19

is usually used on administrative nets, which cover a wider area than tactical nets, and as a back up should VHF communications be jammed, something to which they are more vulnerable than HF.
Ultra High Frequency (UHF) This covers the frequency band 300–3,000MHz and is used for air-to-air and air/ground communications. Since only a limited number of specialist vehicles have UHF sets installed, helicopters will usually communicate with the ground using VHF.

Combat radios are organised into nets. These are a number of radios using the same frequency, which means that they can all speak to and hear one another. Different arms and levels of command will operate in different nets. Thus there will be artillery, army aviation, engineer and infantry/armour dedicated nets, as well as different nets for companies, battalions, brigades and on up through the chain of command to corps level, which is the highest at which combat radio is used. Because many stations need to be on more than one net at the same time, most Western AFVs will carry at least two radios – this is not the case in Warsaw Pact armies, where vehicles below platoon commander level will be equipped with just one radio receiver, without transmitter. Fig 19 shows the lay-out of a typical combat team net. It is commanded by a tank company headquarters and has two tank platoons and a mechanised infantry platoon under command.

The company commander will be concentrating on commanding his company on the company net, but will be listening to what is going on on the battalion net. His second-in-command, on the other hand, will be keeping battalion headquarters informed of what is going on and listening to the

Left:
Combat team radio net.

Below:
The Dutch YPR 765 MICV, armed with an externally mounted 25mm cannon. It was developed by the US firm of FMC as a private venture and is sometimes known as M113½ or, in the Canadian Army, as Lynx. *Netherlands MOD*

progress of the battle at battalion level. If Battalion HQ wants to give the company orders or speak to the commander, the latter will switch to speak on the battalion net, while the 2IC takes over the company net. The HF radios will normally remain switched off unless either the 2IC or company commander needs to pass a message. The supporting arms representatives will also devote most of their attention to what is going on on the company net. Platoon nets are usually used only infrequently, where the platoon has a special task or to provide dismounted infantry with a link to their vehicles.

Combat radio is both vital to the conduct of battle and very vulnerable. Electronic warfare is a major element in modern war, and can be used in three major ways. All stem from the ability of sophisticated equipment to pinpoint the frequency which a particular net is using. Once identified, the enemy can jam it, eavesdrop in order to gain intelligence, or employ deception by joining the net and pretending to be a *bona fide* station on it. In addition, the precise location of stations on the net can be established and physically destroyed by

Below:
Dismounting short of the objective. Note that each British infantry section has a 84mm Carl Gustav recoilless launcher. This will be replaced in time by LAW 80. *Crown Copyright*

means of artillery or air attack. While brigade nets and above, at least in NATO formations, are secure in that the radios have scrambling devices, which means that to any station not having a similar device the transmission appears merely as a heavy carrier wave, nets below this level can be easily heard.

Whether secure or insecure the danger of jamming and physical destruction is very real, but there are measures that can be taken to minimise this. For a start, there is the use of radio silence by units not actually committed to battle. Also of help is to have reserve frequencies which can be switched to when jamming begins. However, there is only a finite number of frequencies available, and the plethora of nets means that most of these are committed. Thus great care must be taken only to use spare frequences when it is essential, so that the enemy does not identify them too quickly. Strict radio discipline is also important, especially keeping transmissions to a minimum. Frequent changes of position also help. On insecure radios much use is made of simple codes when speaking, as well as interrogation methods for discreetly establishing whether suspicious stations are genuine or not.

Top:
US M108 105mm howitzer is still used by a number of European NATO member countries. *Author*

Above:
Harrier GR3 somewhere over the NATO Central Region. *HQ RAF Germany PR*

Electronic warfare is a very complex business, but can be very effective in the anti-armour battle, especially since armour is so reliant on radio communications.

Combined Arms Tactics
On 8 October 1973, the Israeli 190th Armoured Brigade mounted a counter-attack in Sinai with the aim of capturing some of the bridges which the Egyptians had thrown across the Suez Canal to mark the beginning of the Yom Kippur War. The Brigade consisted solely of tanks, a reflection of the Israeli belief in the omnipotence of the tank on the battlefield born of their experience in the 1967 war. They encountered Egyptian infantry armed with the AT-3 'Sagger' ATGW, and the result was that they were cut to pieces before they could close

73

Below:
Another Mowag Piranha variant, this time mounting an Oerlikon 25mm cannon.
Oerlikon Military Products Division

Above:
The BTR-60s clearly indicate that this is a motor rifle division attacking, supported by artillery and fighter ground attack. *Novosti*

with the enemy. They realised their mistake very quickly – the failure to provide infantry support for their tanks.

It is tanks and infantry co-operating closely with one another which provides the workhorse of the modern battlefield. Of course, the supporting arms of artillery, engineers and aviation, both fixed and rotary wing, are vitally important in enabling infantry and tanks to achieve success, but it is the maximum use of mutual support between the two that is the fundamental tactical building block.

Bottom:
Some large German barns can hide a squadron of tanks, as with these Chieftains. While easier to guard than a wood, the disadvantage is that rapid deployment is difficult. *HQ BAOR PR*

Below:
Here, in the face of very light opposition, T-62s attack on their own. Note the use of the tank exhausts to create a smokescreen, a concept which NATO does not use. *Novosti*

Below right:
M2/3 Bradley in a position of observation. *HQ BAOR PR*

In essence, especially in close combat, each can cover the other's vulnerabilities. Traditionally, tanks feared the anti-tank gun most, while infantry, who were generally dismounted, were concerned over machine gun nests. Well concealed anti-tank guns were difficult for tanks to locate, but could be done so by sharp eyed infantry, who could overcome them by fire and movement. The superior firepower of the tank, on the other hand, could neutralise machine guns. Where the country was open, the tanks would lead, while in closer terrain it was the infantry who were in front. In the high speed battle envisaged today, the infantryman will remain in his MICV or APC for as much time as possible, since once he dismounts the momentum of the advance or attack will slow down. Nevertheless, the basic principles of infantry/tank co-operation still apply, and in broken country or in built-up areas, the infantry will continue to lead. If any resistance is expected then they will be forced to dismount.

The MICV, however, has significantly enhanced the infantryman's firepower and he now has less dependence on the tank than in the past. Often, where resistance is light, the infantry can dispense with the tanks to accompany them onto the objective, relying on their MICVs to lay down suppressive fire. The tanks, meanwhile, will remain

Above:
A well-camouflaged MCV-80. *HQ BAOR PR*

off to a flank, enhancing the fire support given by the accompanying MICVs, and will only rejoin the infantry once they have captured the objective and are consolidating in preparation for a possible enemy counter-attack. Where the enemy position is stronger and includes armour, then tanks will play a larger part in the attack, engaging the enemy armour in order to protect the MICVs and APCs.

This leads on to the question as to whether mechanised infantry should, when attacking, dismount short of or on the objective. The Soviet view is that if resistance is light they should not dismount at all, in order to maintain the momentum. If, however, they consider that this will lead to unacceptable casualties to their mounted infantry, then they will dismount some 300m short of the objective and put in the final attack on foot, but led by tanks. Within the NATO alliance there is a divergence of views, and the main difference of opinion is between the British and Americans. The latter believe that, with the hull firing ports in the M2 Bradley IFV, the infantry have sufficient firepower not to have to dismount until they are actually in the enemy position. The British, on the other hand, do not accept the US claim that

accurate fire can be put down to a range of 200m from the Bradley's firing ports when it is on the move. They argue that it is impossible to obtain any degree of accuracy when being pitched about in the back of an APC or MICV moving at speed over rough ground. Rather than run the risk of the vehicle being knocked out at close range by a hand-held anti-armour weapon and killing all the infantry inside, they believe that it is better for the infantry to dismount, and use the combined firepower of the tanks and MICVs to shoot the infantry in. The argument is finally balanced between maintaining the speed of the attack and increasing the risk of casaulties.

Yet, it must not be forgotten that armour and infantry place very heavy reliance on supporting artillery. Fire units must be capable of responding to demands for artillery support at a moment's notice. Two elements enable this to happen. Firstly, artillery is always deployed on the 'leapfrog' principle. While one element is moving to a new fire position, the other is static and ready to fire. A battery cannot afford to carry out too many engagements from the same position because modern artillery locating means are very effective and it will not be long before the enemy has accurately pinpointed it and is bringing down counter-battery fire. Thus, this leapfrogging of fire units will take place very frequently, and is a major

Right:
Europe's first attack as opposed to armed
helicopter, the Italian Agusta A129 Mongoose,
here armed with TOW guided missiles.
Alternatively, it can carry the Hellfire ATGW.
Author

Below right:
Another anti-armour weapon which can be
carried by helicopters is the Oerlikon 25mm, here
mounted on a Bell Iroquois. It is also useful in
the anti-helicopter role. *Author*

Bottom right:
The vulnerability of armed and attack helicopters
when they rise above cover to fire guided
missiles is now being overcome by the
introduction of the mast mounted sight. Here it
is shown above the rotor on a TOW armed
Hughes 530MG helicopter. *Hughes Aircraft Co*

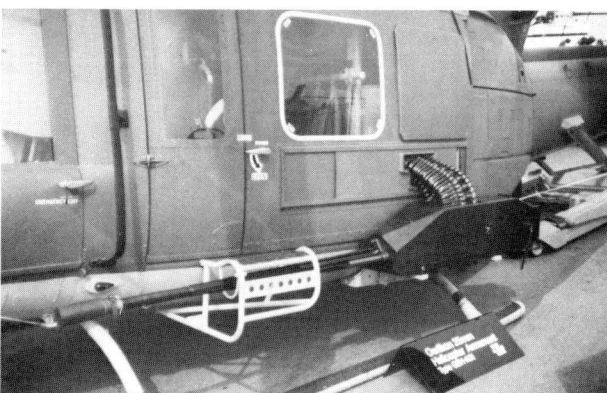

reason why self-propelled artillery is preferred to
towed. The other element is the use of artillery
forward observation officers (FOO) with the
forward troops. They will normally travel in tanks
or APCs, one to each company, and will call down
and correct fire as required. Occasions do arise
when they are not in a position to see the target. In
this event, in NATO armies at least, tank and APC
commanders are trained to direct artillery fire
themselves. By the same token, when the support
of fighter ground attack (FGA) is being used,
infantry and tank units will have the services of
Forward Air Controllers (FAC) to direct it. These
are either Primary, which means that this is their
sole task, or Secondary, – tank or infantry officers
who have received some training in air control
techniques, which means calling in the pilot and
guiding him onto the target.

Concealment and Detection
Apart from physical cover, armour makes much
use of smoke to conceal its movement. Soviet tanks
can generate their own smoke screens, but NATO
armies rely on artillery and mortars to do this,
although tanks themselves do carry a limited
number of smoke rounds. Soviet tanks, on the
other hand, use an additive mixed with the engine
exhaust employing the same principle as the
traditional naval smokescreen. All Western AFVs
also have smoke grenade dischargers fitted. These
provide an almost instantaneous screen of smoke
to cover the individual vehicle should it be fired on
and need to get back behind physical cover before
it is hit. It is interesting to note, however, that the T-
80 MBT is the first Soviet AFV which has them
mounted.

Darkness is the other major cover for movement
and, especially in view of the air threat, major
redeployments always take place at night wherever
possible. There are, nevertheless, a number of

Above:
Blowpipe, the British Army's low level air defence missile. Here it is shown in a new configuration, which takes the weight off the operator's shoulder and gives him the ability to quickly engage other targets. *Short Brothers*

Below:
Javelin, Blowpipe's successor, undergoing firing trials at sea. *Short Brothers*

methods that can be used for locating and identifying armour moving by night. The most elementary is sound, which is amplified at night when the battlefield tends to be quieter than by day. Even so, although an experienced listener can often identify the type of AFV by the distinctive noise of its engine, it is very difficult to pinpoint the location and direction of movement. Thus, increasing use is made of artificial aids.

The first, and oldest, is white light. Both artillery and mortars have illuminating rounds. The round or bomb is designed to burst at a particular height above the ground and releases a flare suspended on a parachute. This can provide illumination over a limited area for some 30–75sec. A problem is that only a limited number of rounds will be available and they will have to be used sparingly. Their use also means sacrificing an element of surprise. White light searchlights mounted on tanks and other AFVs carry the same penalty, besides giving away the position of the AFV. White light can also be used to create what is called 'artificial moonlight' by reflecting it off the clouds and thus raising light levels. Although used to a degree in North-West Europe during 1944–5, it has rather gone out of fashion.

Better than white light, in that it cannot be detected by the naked eye, is infra red. This can be used on two ways. Employed actively, a white light searchlight is used with a black filter and special sights, and these pick up the IR radiations and reflections from the target. It does, however, have

Above:
Low level air defence missile teams will normally ride in APCs. British Army Blowpipe teams use the Spartan APC. *Soldier*

several drawbacks. For a start the range is limited – seldom more than 1,000m – it is affected by smoke, rain and fog, and can be easily detected through an IR sight. It is also very tiring on the eyes to use, and an observer cannot use it for more than 30 minutes at a time. It can be used passively, without the IR beam. Although this prevents detection by the enemy, the effective range is still further reduced. A better system is image intensification (II), which is now replacing IR. It is a passive method and is based on the principle of concentrating the ambient light present even on the darkest of nights. Although its range is no better than active IR, it cannot be detected and the equipment is small enough to be fitted to infantry weapons. It is also used in AFV weapons night sights in conjunction with a thermal pointer. This detects the heat radiated by the target and is not affected by mist and fog. It can also penetrate light foliage and has a greater effective range than II. it can, however,

only detect targets and not locate them, and is not used as a surveillance device on its own. Another system reliant on thermal radiation is called thermal imaging. Using complex equipment, this converts the heat radiated by the target into a pictorial display, sufficiently recognisable as a conventional image. The airborne version of this is called infra red line scan.

Radar, too, is much used on the battlefield. A typical example is the British Radar No 14 Mk 1 or ZB298, which is used by reconnaissance regiments and is able to detect vehicles up to 6,000m and men to 4,000m. It does, however, require much operator training in order to detect particular vehicle types. Being an active system, radar is also detectable. Another technique used is the laser rangefinder. This, however, can only locate, but not identify targets. Finally, seismic alarms, such as the British TOBIAS, can be used to provide early warning. TOBIAS can be set up at range of up to 1,000m from an observation post and connected to it by wire.

With the large number of different types of surveillance system in use on the battlefield at the tactical level, it is essential that some form of night visibility plan is drawn up to co-ordinate their

79

Above:
A typical air defence cannon system in action; in this case the Contraves ATAK-35 demonstrating before the Austrian Army. It is armed with twin 35mm Oerlikon cannon with a rate of fire of 600 rounds per minute. *Contraves AG*

employment. Otherwise, indiscriminate use will result in loss of security and conflict among the various surveillance means. These plans are normally drawn up at brigade or battalion level and typically would break employment of surveillance devices down into three phases. Initially the use of passive means only would be allowed. Then indirect white light – artillery and mortars – and perhaps radar would be permitted in order to begin engaging the enemy without revealing details of the defensive lay-out. Finally, all active systems would be brought into play.

It must be emphasised that the battle does not cease at dusk, and that often there will be more activity by night than by day, especially with the natural cover which darkness brings. Night surveillance aids therefore play a very important part in the anti-armour battle.

Armour and the Air Threat
It was during the last year of World War 2 in Europe that air power began to demonstrate that it could be a grave threat to armour. This was brought about largely by the introduction of the rocket-firing fighter-bomber, and a classic example of how effective it could be was during the Battle of Mortain in Normandy on 7 August 1944. Here Typhoons, Lightnings, Mustangs and Thunderbolts of the 2nd Allied Tactical Air Force played a major part in halting the German counter-attack on the Americans breaking out of Normandy. Since then, with the development of the air-to-surface guided missile and, more recently, the precision guided sub-munition, the threat has increased dramatically.

While ground forces will look primarily to their supporting tactical air forces to keep the enemy air threat off their backs, the air forces themselves, at least during the opening days of hostilities, will be concentrating maximum effort on winning the counter-air battle in order to gain air superiority. This will mainly take the form of attacks against enemy airfields and high altitude dogfights, which will often enable low level ground attack aircraft to slip across the lines unhindered from the air. The same goes for the attack and armed helicopters of both sides. This will place severe restrictions on the employment of armour in that it will, unless actually engaged in battle, need to adopt a low profile. This will mean hiding up in woods and villages and restricting major moves to the hours of darkness. Nevertheless, even when under cover there is still the danger of being attacked from the air. The normal rule of thumb, however, is that if enemy aircraft are seen in the vicinity, they are not engaged with fire unless it is certain that they have identified the position of the armour.

As for the means available to engage fixed and rotary wing aircraft, these come in two types – guns and missiles. At the very low level, that is to a height of 150m, almost all types of AFV have a commander's machine gun, usually 7.62mm, which can be used in the air defence role. More effective are the 20–30mm cannon mounted on vehicles like Scimitar and MICVs. Both, however,

Above:
Saxon passing a Blowpipe position.
HQ BAOR PR

have a problem in acquiring targets. The low flying jet and contour flying helicopter will present themselves only fleetingly to the enemy on the ground, except when a helicopter is firing an ATGW, when it is forced to expose itself at the hover and makes a good target for cannon fire. The speed of the target and the time that it will be in range, especially of small calibre machine guns, will also make it difficult to engage.

At the low level (150–600m altitude) the individual surface-to-air (SAM) missile system comes into play and most armies are equipped with them. The majority, like the Soviet Sam-7 'Grail' and its successor the 'Strela-2', as well as the US Redeye are heat seeking. They are attracted by the heat given off by the aircraft's exhaust and use IR guidance. This means that they are inevitably 'tail chasers' and have to have a high velocity in order

to catch a jet aircraft. They can also be distracted by the use of decoys, usually flares dropped by the aircraft, which the Israelis used so successfully in the Lebanon in 1982. Recent models, such as 'Strela-2' and the US Redeye replacement, Stinger, have higher velocities than their predecessors. Stinger also operates in the ultra-violet, as opposed to infra-red part of the spectrum, which makes it less vulnerable to countermeasures. The British version, Blowpipe, is different in that uses manual line of sight (MACLOS) guidance, which means that it can engage an aircraft at any angle. As operators found in the Falklands, the system is

Above:
Tracked Rapier ready to fire.   *HQ BAOR PR*

somewhat bulky and, while very successful against helicopters and slow flying piston engine aircraft, tracking fast flying jets proved to be difficult. As a result of this, a successor, Javelin, is now being introduced with a more powerful second-stage motor to increase range and semi-automatic line of sight guidance (SACLOS).

There are also a number of very effective gun systems which operate at low level. These are mounted on a tracked chassis and consist of acquisition and target tracking radars coupled with a 20-40mm cannon system. The Soviet ZSU-23-4, German Gepard and US Sgt York are good examples. They are very responsive and are a particular threat to aircraft forced to fly at low level because of the missile threat. The fact that they are on tracks also means that they can accompany armour anywhere. The one army which does not use this type of air defence system is the British, although a few years ago it intended to purchase Gepard, but this was prevented by cutbacks in defence spending.

Above this level, the missile comes into its own again. Between 600-7,500m altitude, which in NATO parlance is termed medium level, wheeled or tracked systems such as the Soviet SAM-8 'Gecko' and SAM-9 'Gaskin', the Franco-German Roland system and US Chaparral are employed. The British also have the combat proven Rapier.

This was combat tested in the Falklands, in the towed configuration, but has now been put on tracks, which makes it much quicker to bring into action and therefore more responsive. Aircraft flying at above this height are unlikely to be a threat to armour and will be dealt with by missile systems positioned further back from the frontline.

Air defence weapons are deployed in two ways. Area defence is covering a formation or unit with general protection, while point defence concentrates on defending a particular location, such as an important bridge, headquarters or ammunition dump. While most systems have an IFF device to differentiate friendly from hostile aircraft, there is always the danger of malfunction and IFF is vulnerable to electronic countermeasures. It is therefore very likely in the heat of battle that any aircraft or helicopter will be engaged by friendly troops. In order to reduce the danger of this, NATO policy is to have three states of defence posture. 'Weapons tight' means that targets can only be engaged on order, and 'Weapons hold' requires positive identification as hostile before opening fire. The third category is only employed when the enemy has overwhelming air superiority. 'Weapons free' means what it implies, that any aircraft can be engaged. Another safeguard is to make aircraft and helicopters fly down precisely designated air lanes over friendly territory.

Having sufficient air defence assets operating with armour does significantly enhance its operational ability and lack of it, combined with an adverse air situation, will severely inhibit it.

82

The Anti-Armour Battle

NATO's Defensive Layout

NATO's policy of forward defence is dependent on having sufficient warning of an impending Soviet attack in order to have the time to prepare defences. Once national governments, operating through NATO's Council of Ministers, have agreed that the threat is sufficiently serious to merit the deployment of troops, this will begin. What is called the 'crash out' is something which in-theatre forces frequently practise, and peacetime barracks can be

cleared within a few hours. Units will normally move direct to hide positions not too far from peacetime locations. Here they will complete their initial logistic replenishment, if this has not been done already. They will then move by night to their deployment positions, which will have already been reconnoitred in detail.

The Covering Force

The first priority for each national corps is to get its covering forces up to the IGB as quickly as possible. It is imperative that they are already in position covering this before the enemy crosses it, since otherwise control of the battle will be lost from the start. The Luchs, Scorpions and Bradley

M3 Bradley *(below)* **and** *(left),* **with twin TOW missile launchers set for firing.** *Author*

M3s will take up a line of observation along the border ensuring that no part is left uncovered. They will be supported by ATGW, helicopters, both observation and attack, artillery and some mechanised infantry and armour. These supporting elements will remain in hides until the enemy actually crosses so as not to give their battle positions away prematurely. Above them surveillance satellites, high altitude reconnaissance aircraft, sideways looking airborne radar (SLAR), remotely piloted vehicles (RPV) and helicopters will be flying missions on the friendly side of the border (apart from satellites and spy planes) to try to gain advance information of when the enemy is about to move.

The Main Defensive Position

The preparation of the main defensive position is the cornerstone of the NATO concept. The more time there is to prepare it, the more solid it will be. There are several elements in its construction.

It is the traditional task of infantry to hold ground, and it is the preparation of their positions which will take the most time. Although all infantry permanently based in the FRG are mechanised, they will not fight the battle in the main defensive position from their vehicles, but on the ground and dug in. While straightforward APCs, which have limited armament, will be of little use in the battle that lies ahead and hence will be left in hides to the rear ready to pick up their infantry when redeployment becomes necessary, MICVs are an important element. Their cannon are effective against light armoured vehicles, especially opposing MICVs and APCs, and the TOW on the M2 Bradley will also be useful against MBTs. The MICVs themselves will not be positioned in and among the dismounted infantry because of the danger of attracting artillery fire, and will normally be off to a flank, again in hides, but prepared to move to pre-prepared fire positions which exploit the range of their weapons to the maximum.

Below:
NATO's main artillery workhorse is the US M109 155mm, here seen in British Army service.
MOD (PR)

Above:
US M110 8in howitzer fires both conventional and nuclear shells. *MOD*

Left:
The US M107 175mm gun is used by NATO armies primarily for counter-battery work. *MOD*

It is the artillery threat which concerns the dismounted infantryman most. The Soviets, as we have seen, have an impressive amount of artillery available and operate it according to three standard norms. These are defined in terms of levels of destruction. Neutralisation is designed to cause minimum damage to the defences, but relies on temporary paralysis during and just after the bombardment. Suppression is the destruction of 25% of men and equipment, while total destruction raises this level to 60%. Where the defence has been well prepared, the Soviets calculate that they will require 200 rounds of 122mm ammunition per hectare (100sq m) to suppress it, but only 150 rounds if it is a hasty defence. This is equivalent to one pound of high explosive per square metre in the latter case and 0.7lb in the former. When British studies of the fighting in NW Europe in 1944-5 concluded that as little as 0.25lb/sq m fired

over a period of 15min, which is the same length of time as the Soviet preparatory bombardment, caused a complete breakdown of morale, the problem facing the NATO infantryman becomes very clear. The answer is to dig deep, but this requires time. Currently, therefore, there are a number of studies being undertaken into efficient mechanical means of constructing shell-proof positions and the use of prefabricated shelters.

In terms of the infantry's dismounted anti-amour weapons. ATGW will, like its mounted counterpart, be sited where it can make maximum use of its range. Hand-held weapons will be positioned as a last ditch defence against opposing tanks and APCs and, in closer country, in ambush positions.

The tanks themselves are also positioned off to a flank and will select fire positions which give good coverage of their areas of responsibility. The positions will often be enhanced by the use of dozer blades, which some tanks have fitted. Again, the tanks will remain in hides until their services are required. Ideally, tanks should be placed where they can overlook a tank killing area. As shown in Figure 20, this is a horseshoe shaped ridge with infantry holding the shoulders. Minefields will channel the enemy armour into it, it is hoped,

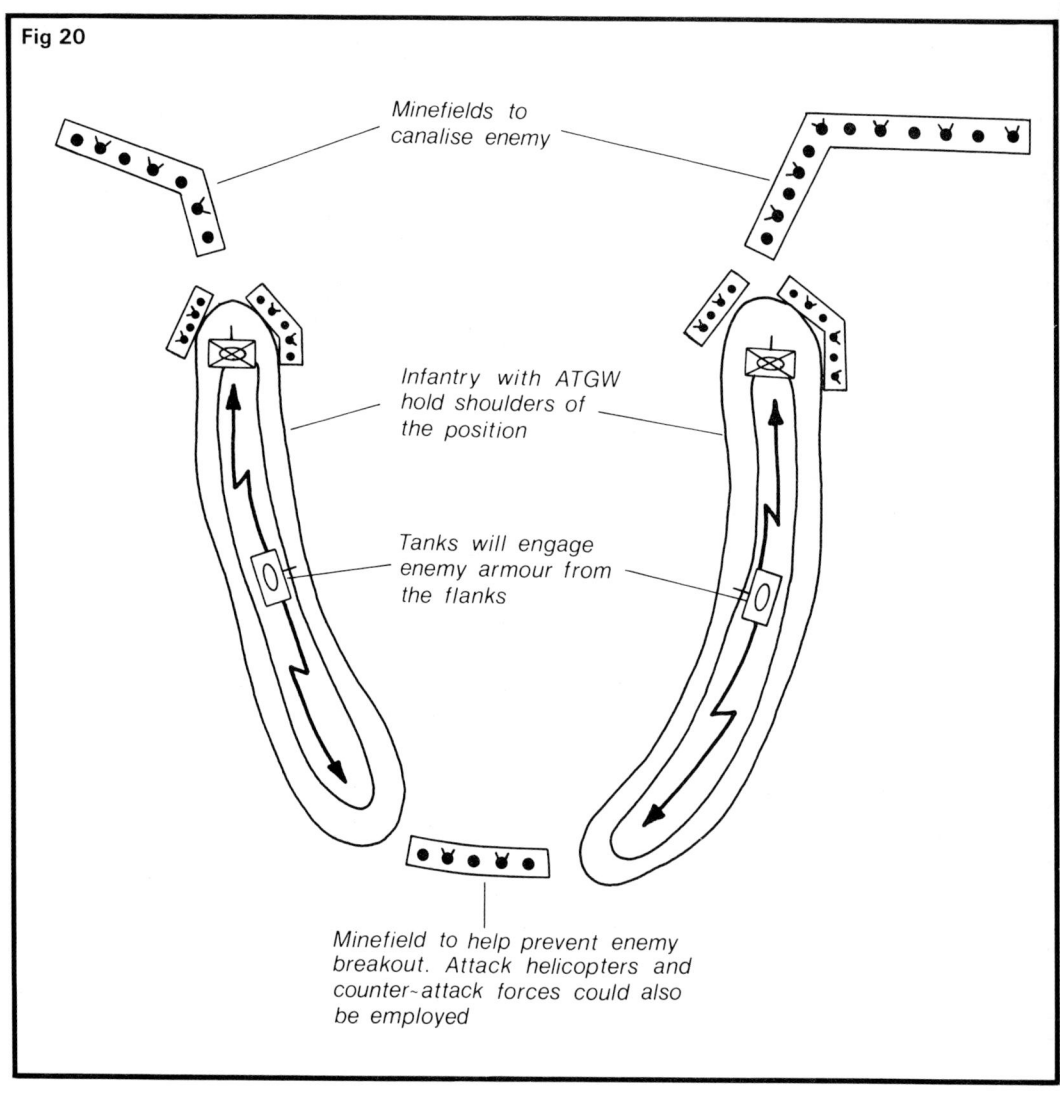

Fig 20

Minefields to canalise enemy

Infantry with ATGW hold shoulders of the position

Tanks will engage enemy armour from the flanks

Minefield to help prevent enemy breakout. Attack helicopters and counter-attack forces could also be employed

canalising the enemy tanks and APCs into the killing area. An important principle in laying out the anti-armour defence is that areas of fire at all levels should be interlocking to ensure that no piece of ground is left uncovered.

NATO doctrine recognises five different types of minefield. Protective minefields are laid close to infantry positions – just out of grenade range – and are often put in by the infantry themselves. Nuisance minefields, on the other hand, are designed to slow the enemy down, being laid in random and scattered groups. There are, too, phoney minefields, which are marked but not laid. The two major types used on the main defensive position are the defensive minefield, which is laid across the enemy's likely axes of advance and designed to break up his attack, and the barrier minefield. As the name implies, the aim of this type is to deny the enemy entry into particular areas, and is the most extensive of the five types. Usually a mixture of anti-tank and personnel mines are used when laying a minefield. All minefields should be covered by fire to make it more difficult for the enemy to clear lanes through them.

Artillery plays a very important role in helping to break up attacks. The 155mm round, which the majority of NATO artillery fires, even though it probably will not achieve a K-Kill on a tank, will when bursting close cause damage to externally fitted items such as radio aerials, as well as destroying sights and giving the crew some concussion. The effect will be even greater on light armoured vehicles. Normally, a number of pre-arranged targets will be agreed. These are known as defensive fires (DF) and the guns will register on

Left:
An ideal anti-armour position.

Right:
A well dug in Milan ATGW. *Soldier*

Below:
A typical dismounted infantryman's anti-tank weapon – the 84mm Carl Gustav recoilless rocket launcher. It has to be carefully sited because of the back blast on firing. *Soldier*

Bottom:
This West German Carl Gustav team are in an ideal position to engage tanks from the flank. *Bundesministerium der Verteidigung*

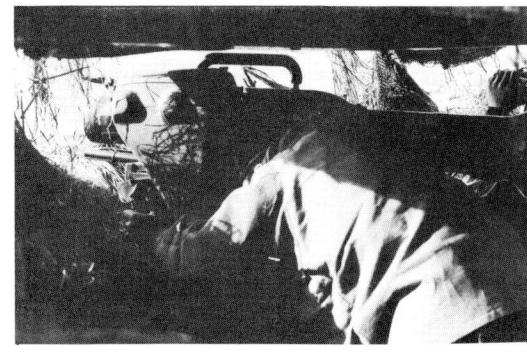

these beforehand and the information necessary for laying the guns accurately on the target will be stored in a fire control computer held at the battery command post. A variant of the DF is the FPF or final preventive fire, a linear target close to the infantry positions, which will be fired if the infantry are in danger of being overrun. Fire is normally controlled by forward observation officers (FOO), who operate with the armour and infantry. They can also call down and correct fire on opportunity targets which are not DFs. There may well be occasions, however, when they are unable to see the target and, because of this, tank and infantry section commanders are trained to do this as well.

Although the defensive battle will be, from NATO's viewpoint, relatively static for a time, once the enemy is across the main obstacle in force it is

likely that he will succeed in penetrating the forward positions. In order to counter this, positions in depth will be prepared. In this context, it is the counter-penetration positions which are seen as vital. These are decided upon at divisional level and based on the enemy's likely plan once he has broken through the outer crust of the main defensive position. Reserve units will be earmarked to occupy relevant counter-penetration positions if a threat is seen to develop, and will have reconnoitred them and the routes to them.

Another asset for countering an enemy break-through through the main defensive position is the attack helicopter. This gives the commander a highly responsive reserve and, rather than fritter it away, he will tend to hold it back until there is a serious emergency. As for fixed wing support, there are two ways in which this can help influence the anti-armour battle. Interdiction attacks beyond the immediate battlefield can disrupt the enemy's second echelon, and close support sorties will be directed against armour formations on the battle-field itself. While interdiction tasks are formulated at the higher levels of command, because only they have the surveillance assets to identify likely targets, close air support missions can be requested at any level. However, because of the numerous demands on combat aircraft, allocation of close

Above left:
British airmobile infantry about to board RAF Wessex helicopters to counter an enemy penetration. *Armed Forces*

Left:
A typical ground attack aircraft, the US Fairchild A-10 Thunderbolt armed with the air-to-surface Maverick missile. *US Air Force*

Top:
The British Lynx helicopter armed with eight TOW ATGW launchers. *Armed Forces*

Above:
Lynx firing TOW. *Westland Helicopters Ltd*

air support sorties will be decided upon at the highest level, Army Group HQ, which is colocated with the headquarters of the Allied Tactical Air Force. It must also be remembered that the primary task of NATO air forces will initially be the counter-air battle, with its aim of maintaining air superiority over the battle area and indeed throughout the Central Region. Because of this, ground force commanders are most unlikely to be granted all their requests for air support.

The Counter-Attack
During the first two phases of the battle it is essential that the enemy does not identify the whereabouts of the armour heavy reserves held at corps and army group level for the main counter-attack. These formations will therefore remain in hides and on radio silence. Most of their time will be taken up with making contingency plans for possible counter-attack tasks, many of which will never be put into practice. Yet, when the moment comes for them to be committed timing will be vital. They will be aiming to hit the enemy armour in the flank, knock it off balance and then destroy it, driving the remnants back across the border. It is crucial that this succeeds. To the rear the out-of-theatre reinforcements from North America and the United Kingdom will still be on the move, that is if the Soviets have succeeded in adhering to their timetable. All that can stop them if the counter-attacks fail are tactical nuclear weapons. Once these begin to be used the dangers of further escalation are only too obvious.

The Battle itself
For those manning the line of observation overlooking the IGB, the period preceding the Warsaw Pact attack will be a tense one. In order to not to give their positions away, they will, like everyone

else, be on radio silence. By day they will use their vehicle sights or dismounted observation posts (OP) to watch the border, while during the hours of darkness II and thermal imaging devices will be brought into play, along with radar. The most likely time for the Soviets to cross the border will be just before dawn, and to do so they will require engineer assistance to cut gaps in the fences, as well as possibly to clear mines, although the minefields along the border are no longer as extensive as they once were, with several having been lifted during the past few years. The deployment of engineer vehicles close to the border will therefore be a useful indicator if it can be identified by aerial reconnaissance.

Making gaps in the border is not expected to take the enemy long – a matter of minutes. Once achieved, his reconnaisance elements will come through and the NATO covering forces, who will have broken radio silence as soon as the enemy has begun to cross, will begin their active phase. The first vehicles which they are likely to see will be BRDMs of the divisional reconnaissance battalions supported by their integral T-64s and BMPs. They will be operating along predetermined axes and it is important that the covering forces both identify these axes and destroy the opposing reconnaissance before it penetrates too quickly and deeply. While the 25mm and 30mm cannon of the M3 Bradley, Luchs and Scimitar, as well as Scorpion's 76mm gun, will concentrate on destroying the BRDMs and BMPs, TOW, Milan and

Swingfire will concentrate on the T-64s, helped, if need be, by attack helicopters.

The NATO covering forces should be able to hold the Soviet reconnaissance, but some of the latter will inevitably slip through the line of observation, especially if it begins to suffer casualties. However, it is more important that they accept this and wait for the leading elements of the main body, for only these can confirm the enemy's intended thrust lines.

The Soviet division, tank or motor rifle, will usually advance on a frontage of some 8km, using two axes with a regiment leading on each and the other two following up as the division's second echelon. The main body may well be preceded by a forward detachment, especially if the divisional

Right:
US HueyCobras stalk enemy armour. They will be helped in this by observation helicopters and will only rise above the treeline to fire their TOW missiles. *US Army*

Below right:
The HueyCobra firing TOW. *US Army*

Below:
Counter-attack and counter-penetration. The enemy could continue his thrust in one of three directions. These can be countered by forces positioned in counter-penetration positions A, B or C. The counter-attacks A, B or C can be made in conjunction with these deployments.

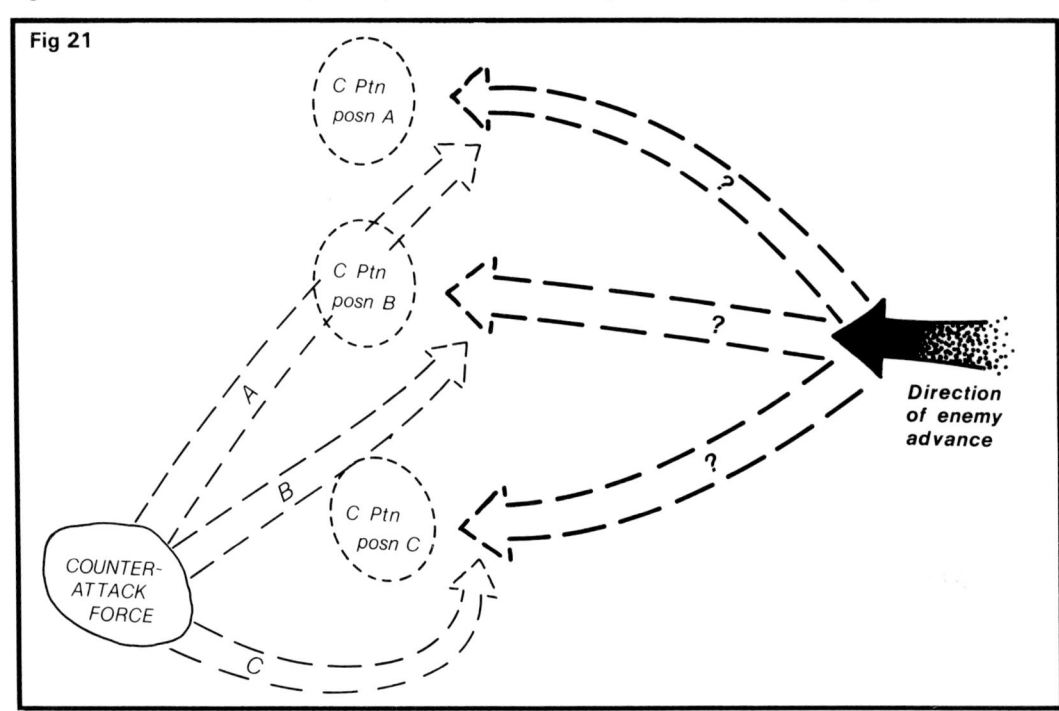

Fig 21

C Ptn posn A

C Ptn posn B

C Ptn posn C

Direction of enemy advance

COUNTER-ATTACK FORCE

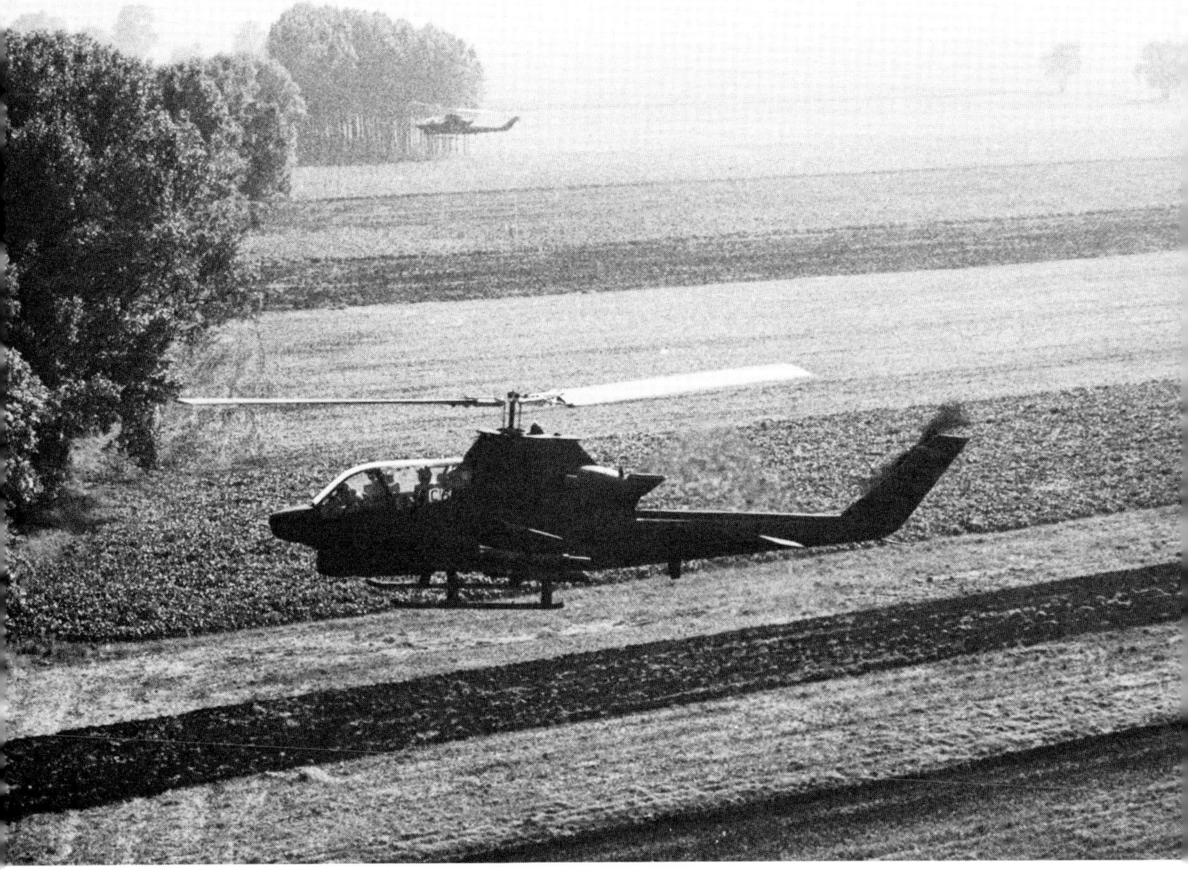

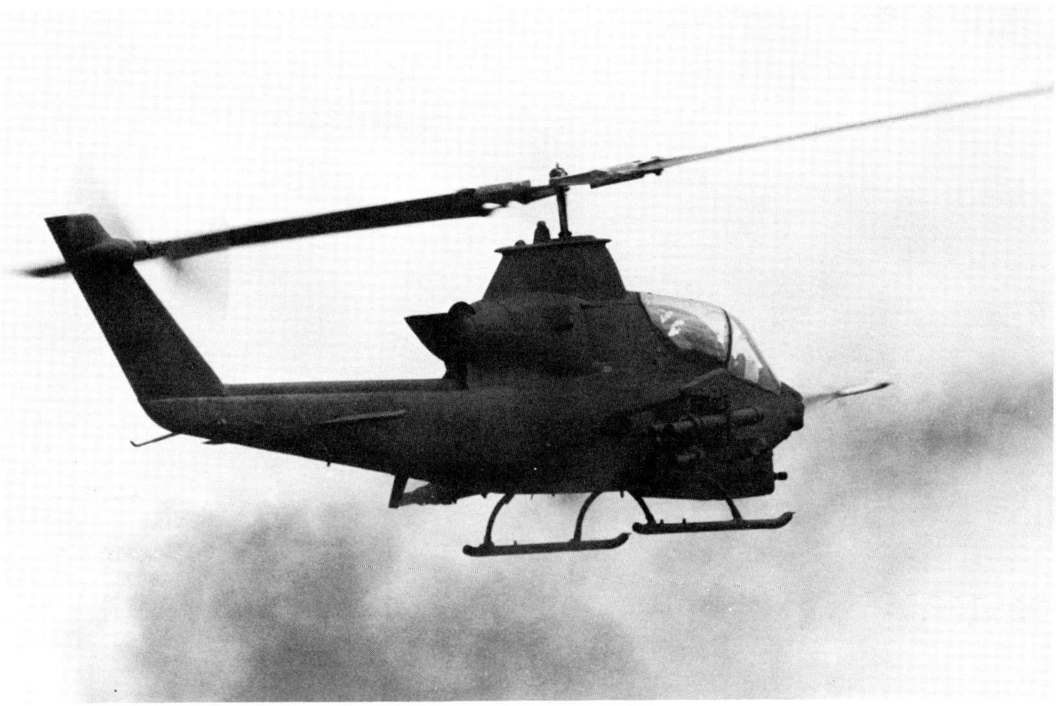

reconnaissance has identified routes through the NATO covering forces. It is stressed, though, that neither the forward detachment nor the main body will deploy from their normal march formation unless they are intending to physically attack enemy positions.

The first indication that the NATO reconnaissance elements will have that the main body is approaching will be a screen of small patrols of one to three BRDMs and BMPs from the regimental reconnaissance companies. Some 5–10km behind them will come the leading battalions. These, as Fig 15 (p. 42) showed, may well be spread out as much as 20–25km in order not to present a nuclear or air target. The NATO covering forces will now fight a delaying action, enticing the opposition to deploy for an attack, and then pulling back to the next bound as the preparatory artillery bombardment begins. ATGW will continue to snipe at long range, ambushes will be set and the enemy's progress also impeded by phoney and nuisance minefields, demolitions on roads and bridges and other obstacles such as tree trunks laid across forest rides. It is, however, vital that the covering forces remain in contact with the enemy throughout. In order to maintain the momentum of their advance, the Soviets will constantly be looking for ways to bypass or infiltrate the NATO

covering forces and, if contact is lost, the Soviet task is made very much more easy.

Nevertheless, the time will come when the NATO covering forces begin to run out of space. They will have by then, it is hoped, gained a clear picture of the main Soviet axes of advance, have inflicted some casualties and perhaps forced the enemy to revise his timetable, as well as gaining additional time for strengthening the main defensive position. Even so, it is not expected that the covering force battle will last more than a day, simply because of the limited depth of the operational area.

Once the NATO corps commanders have decided that their covering forces have done all

Below:
Successor to the HueyCobra, the AH-64 Apache, which is just entering US Army service. *Hughes Helicopters Inc*

Bottom:
Chieftains counter-attack through a smokescreen laid by artillery. *MOD (PR)*

Below right:
For long moves tank transporters are invaluable for saving wear and tear on tanks. This is a Chieftain equipped with a dozer blade for enhancing fire positions. *HQ BAOR PR*

that they can be reasonably expected to do without incurring overwhelming casualties, there comes one of the more difficult parts of the battle. Somehow, the covering forces have got to disengage from the enemy and be got back across the main obstacle to the rear, while at the same time contact must be maintained with the aggressor. The way in which this is done is for the forward divisions, who are responsible for the main defensive position, to put out screen forces, normally a battle group per forward brigade, on the enemy's side of the obstacle and usually a tactical bound in front of it. The covering force will not break clean until it is close enough to the screen for it to be able to cover its withdrawal with direct fire weapons. This having been done, the screen force now takes over the battle while the covering force gets back over the obstacle. Although most of the crossings over the obstacle, which is normally a river, will have already been demolished, a certain number will be kept open. These are termed reserved demolitions and are controlled at the highest level for as long as possible. This will initially be by the corps or divisional commander, and it is essential that they are not blown too early, thus trapping friendly troops on the wrong side, or too late, enabling the enemy to capture them intact. The reserved demolition will have a strong guard on it, usually of

company strength, and the demolition guard commander is given written orders based on a standard form, which spells out the circumstances in which he may or may not order the firing party to blow. As the covering force passes back across the reserved demolitions a careful check will be made that all are across, and then the screen troops will begin their withdrawal. Once they are across on the home bank, the reserved demolitions will be blown.

The enemy's next problem is to get across the obstacle himself. He will, of course, have tried to seize the reserved demolitions, either using a forward detachment or possibly a heliborne force. If he is successful, this might well be the time to launch an OMG. While the Army OMG will support the battle on the main defensive position, seizing vital ground behind it often in conjunction with an airmobile operation, in order to facilitate the subsequent advance as well as forcing the enemy to look in two directions at once, the theatre OMG will strike much more deeply. As described in Chapter Three, its objectives are very much more strategic in nature. Clearly, though, if the Soviets are able to launch an OMG early, it will cause serious dislocation of the NATO defences. Hence it is imperative that during this first phase of the battle which has just been described that the

Left:
T-72 in winter camouflage. *Author*

Below:
M2 Bradley. The only external difference between this and the M3 is that the two firing ports on either side of the hull below the turret are blocked off on the latter. *Author*

Right:
A Soviet T-62 company commander gives out orders to his platoon leaders. This would be an ideal fighter ground attack target, and hence in wartime would be done under cover.
Novosti

various national corps keep in step and do not allow gaps to appear through which an OMG can be sent. This will require close coordination on the inter-corps boundaries.

Assuming, therefore, that the NATO forces have succeeded in deterring the Soviets from launching OMGs, the latter first need to find suitable crossing places over the obstacle. Intelligence gained in peacetime will have given them a very clear idea of where they would like to cross and what the conditions are, but these will still need to be confirmed. Therefore, after last light, engineer reconnaissance teams will reconnoitre the approaches, banks and river bottom. At the same time, the bridges, rafts and assault boats required will be being moved forward. NATO standing patrols on the home bank will do their best to impede the engineer reconnaissance, but very soon the Soviets will get infantry across to establish a bridgehead. The first wave will use assault boats, but will be quickly followed up by BMPs and BTR-60s, which will swim across. Soviet tanks have a schnorkelling capability, and this has been much publicised by the Soviets for many years. Nevertheless, it is questionable whether they will use it to any great extent. It is

known that there is a high degree of risk attached, and in training exercises this operation is only carried out once the river bottoms have been carefully prepared. It is much more likely, therefore, that they will raft their tanks across. This operation of establishing the bridgehead will be carried out under the cover of very heavy artillery fire in order to keep the defenders' heads down. Once the bridgehead is established, the Soviets will set up floating bridges, the PMP which was first employed operationally when the Egyptians used it to cross the Suez Canal in 1973. Speed is now of the essence because, in view of the air

threat, the Soviets will have to dismantle the bridges before first light. Thus, the crossings might take two or three nights to accomplish.

Now that the Soviets are across the obstacle, the crucial part of the battle on the main defensive position takes place. The NATO aim is to contain the Soviet attacks and prevent their armoured columns from breaking out into the country beyond. This must be done by achieving an unacceptable level of destruction, which will force the Soviets to lose momentum. Because the attacker will have a significant superiority in numbers of tanks and other AFVs, it is essential that these are

engaged as early as possible. Ideally, close support aircraft will begin the attrition, guided by FACs on the ground. Then, long-range ATGW (Swingfire and TOW) will begin sniping at enemy tanks between 3,000 and 4,000m. As the T-64s and other tanks come to within 3,000m range, they will be taken on by the M1 Abrams, Leopards, Challengers and Chieftains. At 2,000m medium range ATGW will also be brought into play, and at 1,500m the MICVs will begin to tackle the BMPs and BTR-60s following behind the tanks. Once the enemy have closed to within 600m of the infantry's defensive positions, hand-held anti-tank weapons can be brought into play, while machine gunners and riflemen will prepare for the moment when the Soviet infantry dismount from their vehicles.

This is how the anti-armour battle should be conducted in theory, but in practice it will not be as clearcut as this. For a start, the massive weight of Soviet supporting fire – field artillery, MLRS, attack helicopters and fixed wing air strikes – will seriously degrade defensive firepower, both in terms of destruction and the need to shelter from it. Furthermore, although the increased range and accuracy of modern anti-armour weapon systems would seem to give the defenders a significant advantage, it is more than doubtful that they will be able to exploit this. Battlefield obscuration in

Above:
Soviet infantrymen about to mount their BMP.
Novosti

Below:
The security of bridges in the rear area is vital to NATO if supplies and reinforcements are to keep flowing forward. Here M113s pass a Dutch bridge guard. The sign indicates that the bridge will take an 80 tonne vehicle. *Author*

Right:
What could be the start of a typical OMG operation. While Mi-4 'Hounds' fly overhead to seize vital ground, T-55 crews mount up.
Novosti

terms of smoke and exploding munitions will cut down range considerably. Poor visibility brought about by the weather and nature of the terrain, as discussed in Chapter One, is another limiting factor. Indeed, it is quite possible that most anti-armour engagements will take place at ranges considerably less than 2,000m and often below 1,000m. Certainly this has been the experience in many of the armour clashes in the Middle East, where the terrain is considerably more open than in the Central Region. There is the further danger that the Soviets might well employ as part of their attack preparations chemical weapons, which they regard as a conventional means of waging war. Although many NATO AFVs have collective NBC protection, which means that their crews do not have to wear protective clothing as long as they remain closed down in the vehicle, some like the M2/M3 Bradley do not. For the crews of these and those fighting dismounted the wearing of protective clothing and masks will inhibit their combat effectiveness. A final point is the use of radio

countermeasures (RCM) by the Soviets. The jamming of combat radio nets is likely to be widespread and this will create command and control problems.

Nevertheless, the Soviets, too, will have their

Above:
Soviet tanks schnorkelling across a river. This will only be done when the bottom is very firm and the banks have little slope. *Novosti*

Below:
The most usual method for Soviet armour to cross a river – using the PMP floating bridge. Alternatively, they will be rafted across on an amphibious ferry. *Novosti*

Right:
Logistic resupply is another important element in maintaining the high speed advance. This pipeline system being used by T-55s is ideal for strategic moves, but not on the battlefield, where cans or bowsers will have to be employed
Author

problems. The weight of NATO fire, battlefield obscuration, RCM and the possible chemical environment which they might chose to create, will also hinder them. In addition, their concept of the high speed advance does require much initiative and quick thinking on the part of commanders at the lower levels. In the past, such independence of thought and deed has been actively discouraged and, although they are now making strenuous efforts to instil greater freedom of action among the more junior commanders, there is still a significantly greater rigidity than in the West. As long as events are proceeding according to plan the momentum will be maintained, but, if unexpected opposition is encountered or there is a breakdown in communications, the high speed advance may well peter out. With their fear that NATO might resort to tactical nuclear weapons sooner rather than later, such a slowing down of their rate of advance might be seen as fatal to them and might well tempt them to break their declaration of no first use of nuclear weapons. This will be especially so if they have not succeeded in launching OMGs.

At this stage of the battle the attrition rates on both sides are likely to be high. For the Soviets, this will be the time to begin deploying the second echelon, but NATO, with reinforcements still arriving in theatre and hardly yet ready to be moved forward, will still have to rely on the forces already in place in the main defensive position. They will have by now been fighting for some 48 hours and stress brought on by both the intensity of the fighting and lack of sleep will be beginning to tell. It is therefore now that the Soviets might well achieve a breakthrough with their fresh

second echelon and the third phase of the battle will begin.

NATO army group and corps commanders will have been carefully monitoring the enemy's progress and analysing his likely axes of advance if and once he has broken through the main defensive position. What is most important is that the main axes should be identified from the subsidiaries, so that the main threat can be countered in time. For the Commander-in-Chief Central Europe, this information will enable him to decide whether to deploy III US Corps, which will by now be flying in from the United States, to Northern or Central Army Groups. The army group commanders will need this information in order to position their own reserves correctly, while corps commanders will need it to decide to which counter-penetration positions they should deploy their reserves. Because of the air threat, these will move into position by night. They will normally be infantry 'heavy' and will probably include additional ATGW assets, as well as having attack helicopter support. With their positions sited astride the enemy's axis of advance their object is to halt him. With this done and his momentum lost, it is now the moment for armour heavy counter-attack forces to strike him in the flank, supported again by fixed and rotary wing aircraft. This is where the shock effect of NATO armour can really be brought into play, and it is hoped that the resultant destruction of the enemy's material and plans will force him to halt and begin to withdraw.

The Effect of the OMG

The description above has presupposed that the enemy has been unable to launch OMG, either at army or theatre level. It also assumes that NATO has had sufficient warning time to be able to occupy and prepare the main defensive position. If, however, the Soviets have been able to achieve sufficient surprise to clash with NATO forces while they are still deploying, the meeting engagement to which they aspire above all else, then the battle will be very much more fluid and the opportunities to use OMGs that much greater.

The effect of an OMG of one tank division operating in the rear of a NATO corps' still ill-prepared defensive positions might well be far-reaching. Its most likely target would be the seizure of important bridges on main supply routes. Besides giving a springboard for the advance subsequent to the battle on the main defensive position, it would also gravely hinder the deployment of troops to the main defensive position and the passage of supplies. The corps commander would also be forced to fight a battle in two opposite directions and would be forced to commit at least some of his reserves much earlier than he would wish. Indeed, there is a danger of them being dissipated in attempting to contain and destroy the OMG.

The theatre level OMG, with its three divisions, can – apart from destroying tactical nuclear missile sites – cause much dislocation of NATO command, control and communications (C^3) assets by attacks on headquarters, communications centres and the very fact that it is operating so deep in the rear. Both types of OMG will often be used in conjunction with airmobile or, in the case of the theatre OMG, airborne forces. These will seize vital points and hold them until reinforced by the OMG. Special forces *(Spetsnaz)* teams and fifth columnists will also operate in support of OMGs,

Above:
The counter-attack gets underway. Chieftains supported by a Lynx attack helicopter armed with TOW. *Armed Forces*

Left:
The maintenance load on tanks can be very heavy in the field. Here an FV434 assists in an engine change on a Chieftain ARV. *HQ BAOR PR*

providing intelligence and sabotaging the efforts of NATO force deployments designed to eradicate them.

Nevertheless, there are ways in which the OMG can be countered. For a start, once identified, reconnaissance elements, both air and ground, must keep close contact with the OMG, and it must be continuously harried. In particular, it takes its own logistic slice with it and, if this can be destroyed, the OMG will soon grind to a halt. In terms of counter-penetration, NATO airmobile forces are, in view of their ability to react and deploy quickly, invaluable. However, the selection of an effective counter-penetration position will be critical, since the OMG will try to bypass rather than fight, since speed is of the essence in reaching its ultimate objective. The position must therefore be dominating enough to force the OMG to take a wide detour. It is at this time, when it has been forced to change direction that a counter-attack will be most effective.

SEVEN

The Future

Many commentators consider that NATO's current doctrine of defence in the Central Region suffers from two main disadvantages. Because of the Warsaw Pact's heavy superiority in numbers of men and conventional weapons, there is a fear that there is too much of a reliance on tactical nuclear weapons as a force multiplier and that NATO will be forced to use these sooner rather than later. Allied to this is the concept of forward defence itself. It is understandable that the host nation should want to ensure that every inch of her territory is defended, but by laying out the main defensive position so far forward and maintaining a policy of not allowing any preparation of it in peacetime, NATO troops have little room in which to fight and very limited time to make the main defensive position anything like secure. This is seen to play into Soviet hands in making early penetration by both OMGs and echeloned main forces that much more likely.

In order to improve NATO's chances, one school of thought advocates a more positional type of defence relying on preprepared fortifications. They argue that the construction of a network of NBC-proof strongpoints along the Inner German Border would in itself be a deterrent to possible Soviet aggression, but would also make it very much more difficult for quick penetration to be achieved. On the surface this seems an attractive proposition, but there are some grave disadvantages. For a start, the Federal Republic's constitution does not recognise two Germanies, and defences of this nature would be tantamount to doing just this. Furthermore, it lays down that there must be unrestricted access for civilians across the border, which such a fortified line would prevent. Economically, the cost of setting up such a comprehensive system is likely to be high, and also the Soviets could make much propaganda value out of it. Militarily, it would commit NATO to one very rigid defence concept which would be impossible to alter in the future.

Nevertheless, there are counter-mobility preparations which NATO could make in peacetime, which would help to canalise the enemy. The Israelis, for instance, use an anti-tank obstacle called a 'fish pond'. This a concrete lined trench with dragon's teeth set in it, which is then filled with water and is stocked with fish in peacetime. The slopes of hills can be made steeper in order to make them inaccessible to tanks. Drainage ditches can be constructed in such a way as to make them anti-tank ditches and tree plantations be laid out in 'no go' areas. There is also the growing urbanisation of West Germany which, in itself, acts as a brake on movement. Discreet strengthening of cellars and houses in the villages to make them into effective strongpoints would be a benefit, and they could be held by local German territorial forces. Anything which can be done in peacetime, without upsetting host nation susceptibilities, to hinder the enemy's mobility and therefore lessen the chances of the quick victory for which he strives, is to strengthen NATO's military position in the Central Region.

The other main concept is very much US generated and takes a very different view. Its foundation lies in the lack of depth which NATO forces have forward in which to operate. Accepting that, for political reasons, forward defence cannot be changed, the Americans argue that the battlefield can be extended on the enemy's side of the border. This has been enshrined as official US Army doctrine in the 1982 edition of their manual FM100-5, and is called 'AirLand Battle'. In essence, they see the key to Soviet success as being the follow-on echelon. If the first echelon can be held and the second destroyed before it can add its weight to the attack, a Soviet offensive will fail. AirLand Battle itself is essentially a US Army doctrine, which views NATO reserves being deployed to counter-attack across the forward edge of the battle area to strike at Soviet forces when they are at their most vulnerable. There are, however, a number of variations on this doctrine. Army 21, which was previously called AirLand Battle 2000, is designed for the period 1995–2030, and uses several emerging technologies in what is

Top and above:
The American AFVs for the future: M1 Abrams MBT and M2 Bradley MIW. *Both Michael C. Klewer*

envisaged as a highly fluid and lethal battlefield. Follow-on force attack (FOFA) is the brainchild of SACEUR, General Bernard Rogers, and argues that Warsaw Pact forces should be located and harried from the air the moment they leave their barracks. Unlike Army 21, he does not envisage ground troops penetrating Warsaw Pact Territory.

AirLand Battle implies reliance on help from the US Air Force, which, while it accepts the principle, has not as yet adopted it as doctrine. The major stumbling block is the control of air assets. While the Army would like to see these parcelled out to the corps, the USAF argues that air power is most effective when controlled centrally. Nevertheless, the USAF does have a deep attack doctrine called 'Deep Strike'. This incorporates 'Assault Breaker', which is based on the use of smart munitions carried by surface-to-surface missiles and aircraft to strike mobile targets such as tank formations, and 'Counterair 90'. As this implies, it reflects the Air Force's view that until the counter-air battle is won it will be unable to give much support to the ground forces. Its cornerstone is the destruction of fixed targets such as airfields, using surface-to-surface and air-to-surface missiles, as well as unmanned aircraft.

All these concepts come under the general term of 'Deep Attack'. As yet none have been formally

accepted by NATO. Among the European members there is a feeling that, in their offensive nature, they run against the whole essence of NATO which is a strictly defensive alliance. Their dependence on sophisticated technology also implies a sharp increase in defence expenditure, which many members are doubtful that they can afford. Militarily, too, they rely heavily on highly efficient C^3I systems capable of producing real-time intelligence which can be acted on quickly. Although the automation produced by the ever increasing use of battlefield computers might seem to make this possible, the very much greater volume of information flow, together with the ever present problem of the 'fog of war', may in practice make this difficult to achieve. The Americans, however, accept that the concept is as yet in the early stage and that it will need much refining once all the various possible problem areas have been investigated in depth.

It is clear, though, that emerging technology is going to have a far-reaching effect on the anti-armour battle. The advent of the PGM, in particular, will present the tank with perhaps its greatest threat yet. The aspect which causes greatest concern is that vertical attack PGMs such as Copperhead and the precision-guided mortar threaten the tank's top armour. In the past this has always been one area in which designers have saved weight by making it thinner than the front, sides or belly. Most experts consider that the MBTs of today have reached their zenith in terms of weight and size. In any event, the need to up-armour the front sides of

Below:
Another view of Challenger. *Author*

the turret with Chobham style armour has made it even more of a target than before, and to place additional armour on the turret top and engine decks would merely aggravate the problem.

The next generation of MBTs is therefore likely to be considerably smaller. This will be achieved by placing all the crew in the hull, thereby removing the requirement to have a large turret. The main armament will be externally mounted using an autoloader, which means that the crew on Western tanks will be reduced to three men, or even two, a possibility which the French are seriously considering for their main battle tank of the 1990s, *Engin Principal de Combat.* The gun itself may remain as a 120mm smoothbore, or be of reduced calibre. The Americans, for instance, are currently trialling a 75mm gun made by ARES of Cleveland. This is a high velocity gun designed to fire long rod penetrators in bursts or single shots. One problem with the externally mounted gun is over crew optics. If the crew are restricted to the hull, their field of vision is very much more restricted than if they are in a conventional turret. The technological solution to this rests in recent advances in optronics and fibre optics, and envisages remote surveillance devices mounted on the hull roof with the crew using a television screen. Clearly, this is not as satisfactory as being able to check the ground with the naked eye, and there are doubts as to whether the crew will be able to acquire targets so quickly. One possible solution to this is the raisable gun, using an extendable periscope. The commander can therefore offer the very minimum target when

he is observing, and merely raises the gun when he wants to fire. The Swedes are investigating this idea as part of their UDES-17 project.

In terms of the tactical handling of armour, the growth of ATGW on the battlefield has already meant that less tanks have to be deployed in the 'shop window' in the defensive anti-armour battle. The advent of PGMs is likely to accelerate this process, and no longer will the MBT be the primary anti-armour weapon. For NATO this will mean that the tank will not be so obvious on the battlefield. Nevertheless, it can still play a decisive part. Armour will spend much more time in hides waiting to carry out the counter-stroke. When it does so, the action will be short and sharp, relying on surprise and momentum to produce the necessary shock to throw the enemy off balance. Its task done, it will then retire once more to its hide.

For the attacker, the problem is more difficult – reliant as he is at present on armour to give him the quick conventional victory for which he strives. Because armour in the advance or attack must necessarily expose itself more than in defence, PGMs offer an even greater threat to him. It may be, therefore, that the Soviets will place increasing reliance on airmobile operations to disrupt the NATO defences, with their armour doing quick dashes in order to achieve the link-up. Whatever doctrine is finally adopted by both sides, there is no doubt that emerging technology is forcing a radical reappraisal of the traditional *modus operandi* of armoured warfare.

NATO and Warsaw Pact Tactical Symbols

Fig 22 **NATO and Warsaw Pact tactical symbols.**	NATO	Warsaw Pact
Division command post		
Brigade/Regimental command post		
Battalion command post		
Company command post		
Mechanised infantry platoon command post		
Tank Platoon commander		
Mechanised infantry platoon		

Tank company		
Mechanised infantry battalion group		
Rifle squad/section		
Reconnaissance element		
Observation post		
Light MG		
Heavy MG		
Anti-tank gun		
Mortar		
Artillery gun		
MBT		
APC		
Wheeled vehicle		

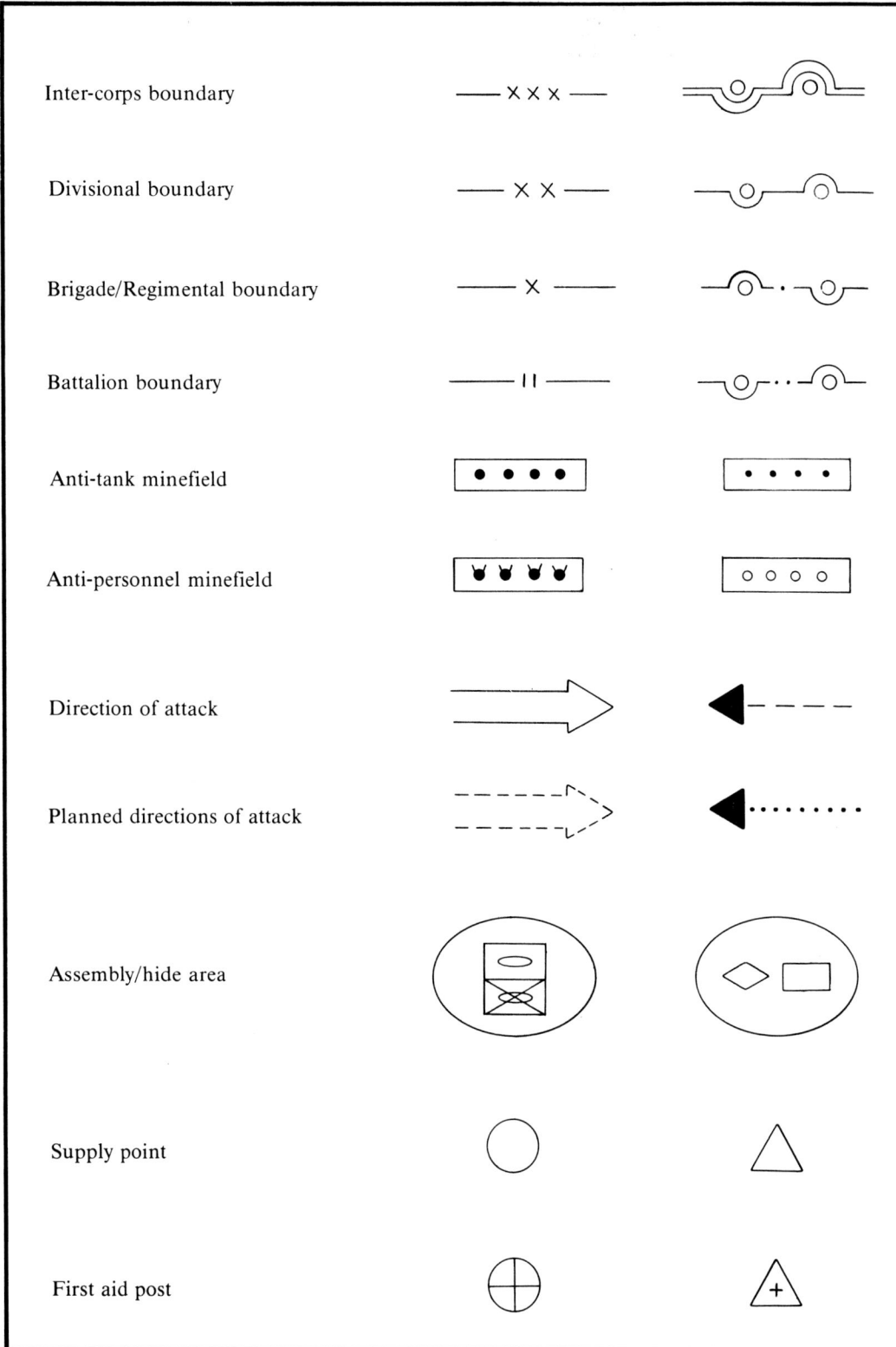

Inter-corps boundary

Divisional boundary

Brigade/Regimental boundary

Battalion boundary

Anti-tank minefield

Anti-personnel minefield

Direction of attack

Planned directions of attack

Assembly/hide area

Supply point

First aid post